UNFAIR COMPARISONS

NUANCING THE "SOLD, NOT BOUGHT" CATEGORY

Empowering your teams to close the gap between consumer perceptions and industry intentions

MARIA FERRANTE-SCHEPIS

Published by InnoGage Publishing
Warrenton, Virginia
www.innogagency.com/publishing
InnoGage Publishing is a registered trademark of InnoGage Holdings, LLC.

ISBN: 979-8-9923348-0-7 Hardcover
ISBN: 979-8-9923348-1-4 Paperback
ISBN: 979-8-9923348-2-1 Ebook
LCCN: 2025900768

Printed in the United States of America.

Publisher's Mission: InnoGage Publishing is passionate about empowering authors to share their unique voices and bring impactful ideas to life. We specialize in transforming concepts into beautifully crafted books that inspire, captivate, and resonate with readers around the globe. If you're ready to turn your manuscript or book idea into something extraordinary, we'd love to hear from you.
Visit us at www.innogagency.com/contact-us to get started.

TABLE OF CONTENTS

FOREWORD

When Maria asked me to write the foreword to *Unfair Comparisons*, I enthusiastically replied, "Of course," because of our friendship and my admiration for her insights into sales, marketing, and human nature, specifically as it relates to the life insurance field.

Maria Ferrante-Schepis has the best sales savvy of anyone I know—and I've been in the life insurance industry for fifty-eight years! She has applied thoughts, insights, song lyrics, humor, and images to concepts we've encountered and feared. As she has extensively written, life insurance is in a "sold, not bought" category, and simply giving those words voice has provided us with valuable appreciation from the industry. Now, *Unfair Comparisons* creates its own two-way exchange (a term she defines later in the book) between the reader and Maria herself, an important thought leader on the issues affecting the life insurance industry. When I read the book, I heard her voice as I read it.

I particularly appreciated the central themes of *Unfair Comparisons*—such as that of oranges and apples, or in the case of life insurance and other categories, oranges and socket wrenches! The book resonates with me regarding the challenges and opportunities of helping people explore what they truly want, even when they haven't yet identified what matters to them.

I've encountered all the excuses: "I have plenty," or "I don't need it"—not to mention, "Don't call me again!" I recognized that the rejection wasn't personal; fundamentally, they were avoiding the discomfort of the topic *(I hope it was just the subject, not me!)*.

In Chapter 4, Maria refers to authenticity as the intersection of your passion, professionalism, and personality. As she is one of the most authentic people I know, she certainly has the right to define it. She offers wisdom, which I like to define as the meeting place of knowledge and experience, to her readers.

After reflecting on my personal experience (and passion), I've realized that life insurance agents face fewer regulated obligations to their clients than in most areas of financial services. While a fiduciary must serve the client with skill, diligence, prudence, knowledge, and loyalty—making only suitable recommendations in the client's best interest—none of these standards are required in forty-nine of the fifty states that regulate insurance agents. The challenge, then, is to distinguish oneself by embodying these qualities based on one's own ethos—and market savvy—to stand out in a crowd where these attributes are not required. I believe Maria speaks to the same outcome, though perhaps through slightly different means. I recommend you take the time to explore your discoveries in the "cheat sheet" provided in the book.

One of my favorite metaphors I have heard Maria and her colleagues at Maddock Douglas say is, "You can't read the label when you're sitting inside the jar." That phrase helps us recognize that we all have blind spots and gives us the constant challenge to think differently about almost everything!

The memory that has stuck out most in my mind about Maria and how she can reinvent our way of thinking was the phone call I received from her in mid-2007 while I was driving on the highway after a meeting. When I knew it was Maria, I pulled off to the side of the road for my own safety, knowing that there'd be a new idea coming. That 1-1/2-hour call gave birth to **Life Insurance as an Asset Class**, one of my favorite collaborations. "LIAC" and the connection between us spans almost 20 years. She references it later in the book as one of the real-life applications of reframing a problem. And it worked.

As Maria ends this book, I will similarly end this foreword, "...hoping that whatever impact you are intending to make in this industry, that you feel strong and confident about achieving it. More power to you! Let's make the future of the industry as vibrant and valuable as we can, while we still can!"

RICHARD (DICK) WEBER. MBA, CLU, AEP
Founder, The Ethical Edge, Inc.
A 58-year veteran ...and still learning!

ACKNOWLEDGMENTS

I would like to thank all the people who contributed, directly or indirectly, to the creation of this book. It is steeped in the work of my colleagues at Maddock Douglas over many years, particularly Mike Maddock, who has always encouraged me to write about what I believe in and share it with the world.

Some of the brightest minds at Maddock Douglas pioneered the various studies and frameworks referenced in this book, including Gino Chirio, Luisa Uriarte, Cindy Malone, Mindy Predovic, Chrissy Zahn, Stephanie Savage, Wes Douglas, Doug Stone, Randy Simms, Cassie Slimmer, Lauren Schwartz, and many others. None of this insight would exist without the brave work of our many clients in the insurance industry—each with a unique perspective on the challenges—and their willingness to take risks to create positive change.

I would also like to thank Steve D'Annunzio and Raeanne Lacatena for their generosity of time and knowledge on the important topic of fear management, which I believe has the power to truly transform an industry in need of a new training paradigm. Thank you to Danielle Swann and Bonnie Godsman for quickly turning this idea into action.

A big thank you to Jon Kia, Corinne Weaver, Kaitlin Travis, and the InnoGage team for their incredible support during the process of writing, editing, and packaging this book. Thank you to my brother, Mike Ferrante, for the cover photography.

I'd also like to thank Paul Umbach, Terri Hill, Tasha Jo Hill, and the talented team at Square Planet for their help with the initial prototype of this work, which, believe it or not, began as a musical. That work helped me recognize my own strengths and "fail forward" in the right direction. *(Who knows? Maybe those songs will reappear in some way down the line. :))*

Thank you to my family and friends for being supportive and understanding when I needed to retreat to my office and think. This section would not be complete without expressing my deep gratitude for the love and support of my husband, Jim. He not only understands my perspective but also shares a unique lens as a veteran of the industry for four decades. His opinion is one I deeply trust and respect. It is through him, and the opportunity to work with the people at Lifetime Financial Growth, that so many of these nuances and lessons have become more than just theory.

Finally, thank you to all the musicians who wrote the amazing songs I've carefully chosen to quote in this book. Regardless of what their original intentions for these lyrics may have been, to me, they hold deep meaning. They serve as a reminder to all of us to stay true to what is most important.

INTRODUCTION

I am pleased to release my second book on a subject that's near and dear to my heart, but not necessarily well understood by a large portion of the population. If you are reading this book, you are most likely passionate about the insurance industry and advancing its true mission.

I've stated time and again that before I leave this Earth, I'd like to have had some impact on closing the gap between the insurance industry's true intentions and the consumers' perceptions.

While this book is relevant to all of the insurance industry and other, broader financial services, the "sweet spot" is life insurance. It's where I got my start, it's what inspired my desire to strengthen my problem-solving skills, and it has taken up a significant amount of my brain space since I first joined.

This book is a sequel to *Flirting with the Uninterested; Innovating in a "Sold Not Bought" Category,* co-authored with Mike Maddock. I was very pleased with how well the industry received that book, and many people said they were motivated to innovate. This news was certainly thrilling.

Now, with another twelve years under my belt, and after observing how the pace of change has impacted the industry, I feel it's time for greater understanding and connection to the people we are serving. Nuance is key.

Let's define nuance before we go any further. Nuance means subtlety. It's about making distinctions that can often be overlooked or even outright ignored. If I have learned anything in the last decade, I have learned that nuance, and the ability to detect it, is one of the most important skills for success.

Nuance means that there are multiple layers of detail, and each one is important. Everyday examples include things like music, wine, and food. Learning nuance in these spheres of life would mean learning the differences between what's okay, good, and "OMG, fantastic!" Some people are skilled at detecting these differences. Others don't sense them as much, and they are just as happy to have that chicken parmigiana from the local pizza place as they are eating in the five-star restaurant. Honing this skill is not about passing down judgment of what's right or wrong. If you like the $12 bottle of wine, buy it. *(I like some inexpensive wines myself, perhaps because my palate isn't super sophisticated.)*

However, if our industry truly desires progress, we must become more sophisticated connoisseurs of the finer details. While this book contains many subtle, and not so subtle, nuances that I believe are important, there are likely many more to discover and discuss. It's less about you "adopting" my definitions of them, and more about exercising the muscles that help you become attuned to them for yourself.

One of the most important nuances is the notion of **unfair comparisons**. As you'll read later, this concept has much to be learned and explored. We must remember the nature of demand and how life insurance requires a **cultivation of demand**. We know this point intellectually, but many still want the demand for life insurance to be the same as other products.

It's not, nor should it be. And that's okay. There's much to be learned by not trying to force life insurance to be fashionable and glamorous, but rather by recognizing what we can change and leaning into improvements.

That said, this book comes along with a series of suggested experiments, explorations, and also a few things I would consider "imperatives"—things that will get you better results if you invest in them. If you do nothing else but embark on these imperatives in an open-minded, curious, "no agenda" sort of way, you and your teams will develop the senses of a connoisseur of insurance innovation. I hope you'll do it!

DEDICATION

This book is dedicated to the memory of my best friend forever, Kristin Valerga Goetze (1965-2023).

Kristin and I met when we were both three months old. Because our houses were backed up against one another's, our families were (and still are) very close. She and I shared every life event imaginable, including kindergarten, elementary school, junior high, high school and college graduations, weddings, the birth of her children, and everything in between. Then, we shared the experience of preparing for her passing from cancer at the age of fifty-seven.

While I didn't make my living as a life insurance agent, she knew that I was someone who could give her advice about it. When she got married and started having her family, I advised her to take out a larger policy than she may otherwise have. She was frugal and never "wasted" money on things she didn't see value in, and the idea of such a large amount of money being "needed" in the event of her death seemed excessive to her. However, with a little coaxing and gentle pressure to help her see how much she was really worth as a breadwinner in her family, she agreed. She resisted some of the underwriting requirements, thereby looking to continue putting it off, but again, I kept the gentle pressure on until the job was done. That was a good fifteen years prior to her illness, maybe even more.

When it became clear that she was in the last few weeks of her life, I dreaded the possibility that she might have let go of that policy without telling me. Perhaps she was one of those people who just decided "I really don't need this." I got up enough guts to ask and learned that it was, in fact, still in effect. Thank goodness. Her husband was way too distraught to go to work for several months. At the time, they had one son in his first year of college and the other one still in high school. That money helped them to feel financially secure while their world was turned upside down.

In my forty-plus-year career in this industry, I've probably been involved with the sale of less than ten policies *(directly, that is).* I've already seen two of them pay out. My dad's policy was the other one. The impact is significant and life changing. In many ways, it saves other people's lives.

For all of you out there who have secured coverage on hundreds, or even thousands, of people, you're doing such a good thing. Thank you for your perseverance, your willingness to be vulnerable to the word "no," and for the impact that you have made, and will continue to make, on so many people. For those of you who bring new people into this business, your impact is magnified a hundred times.

Keep up the great work, everyone, and don't forget to be human.

CHAPTER ONE

THE INDUSTRY'S REAL SUPERPOWER (HUMAN VS. ANIMAL)

"And I'm here, to remind you / Of the mess you left when you went away / It's not fair, to deny me / Of the cross I bear that you gave to me / You, you, you oughta know."

–ALANNIS MORISETTE,

"You Oughta Know," 1995

This song isn't really relevant to this topic, but the words in the chorus are. Because when people leave your life, it can be a mess. It's not fair, and I think you should know.

That said, everything I needed to know about life insurance, I learned from my childhood cat.

You might be wondering what a cat has to do with life insurance. You see, watching our family cat give birth to her kittens was a fantastic, prominent experience of my young life. Seeing them come into the world, naming them, and eagerly awaiting them to open their eyes so I could play with them formed some of my best early memories.

Figure 1: From survival of the fittest to the sharing economy

So, imagine how devastated I was at the sight of a tiny kitten curled up in a corner, his body seemingly lifeless with his tongue hanging out. That's how I found Boots, the runt of my cat's litter, one morning when I was seven years old. It was a moment of sheer panic for me. I screamed for my dad, who came running, despite his general aversion to cats, because he knew how much I cared about them.

My dad, who could fix almost anything, promised me that he would help Boots. Though his words reassured me, I remained worried. Boots appeared to be dead, but my parents sent me to school with the promise that everything would be alright. My skepticism grew with each passing hour until I came home to discover that Boots was, indeed, *okay*.

My dad had managed to revive him by spoon-feeding him milk, massaging his belly, and taking him to the vet for proper care. The mother cat had initially kicked him aside, believing he was too weak to survive. She was following an instinct to conserve resources for the healthier kittens.

This moment was more than just a dramatic episode of my childhood; it was a lesson in the importance of empathy and the spirit of what separates humans from animals. Unlike the mother cat's harsh but natural decision to reject the weak and favor the strong, **humans generally strive to support the less fortunate.** We create systems—both formal and informal—to help those in need, from charities and welfare programs to crowdfunding platforms (part of the sharing economy) and community initiatives. These systems reflect humanity's collective commitment to ensure that everyone has a chance to thrive, especially when they are vulnerable. To accomplish that goal, they pool resources to do it. After all, utilizing the power of many is a smart and effective way to help the few who need it. This determination to help others is the insurance industry's real **superpower.**

What happened to Boots, you may be wondering? We had to make him healthy again if he had any hope of ever rejoining his siblings and his mother. The vet taught us how to bottle feed him, and before I knew it, he was thriving. So much so that the mother cat even took him back. This story, as dramatic and traumatizing as it could have been, had a very happy ending.

So, as we uncover the finer points of what's now referred to as the sharing economy and how it connects to life insurance as an industry, think of Boots and the empathy that drove my family and I to save him. It's a powerful reminder that the essence of sharing is not just in the act itself but in the underlying compassion that fuels it.

WHAT DO KIDS KNOW ABOUT INSURANCE? NADA

How old were you when you first seriously considered the topic of life insurance? For me, I had just turned eighteen. I had stumbled into the insurance industry quite by accident. In fact, my entry into this field was so serendipitous that it almost feels like a case of cosmic alignment. At the time, I had no preconceived notions about insurance because I had zero understanding of the industry. That turned out to be a surprising advantage.

By that point, I had heard the word "insurance" often enough—it sounded important because my parents talked about it on occasion, and I saw it mentioned on TV several times. It was a common term in the adult conversations I overheard, but I had no real understanding of what it meant or how it worked.

The year was 1984, and I was attempting to figure out my future. Having temporarily left college to get my life back on track, I found myself on the hunt for a job. My parents were clear: if I was living under their roof, I needed to contribute. So, I scoured the job market, but my lack of a degree and experience narrowed my options. However, since it was the early 1980s, that meant that I could leverage my technological skills on a computer to bolster my career and create a future for myself. I was still in that gray area, however *(between the boomer meme "Old Economy Steve" and Gen X persona Alex P. Keaton)*.

Figure 2: Alex P. Keaton, played by Michael J. Fox in the TV series called Family Ties. And the internet meme, Old Economy Steve.

My search led me to apply for various positions—receptionist at a doctor's office, administrative clerk at a broadcasting company—but my lack of job experience and, perhaps, my lack of interview skills kept me from landing any of those roles. Just as I was about to give up hope, a small life insurance company offered me a glimmer of opportunity. I was initially seeking a position as a file clerk, but when I arrived for the interview, I was told that the position had been filled. *(Darn, all I needed to know was the alphabet!)*

However, the company had an opening for an "illustrations clerk," a role that I thought required artistic skills. When I was told that drawing was not part of the job description, I learned that it involved creating insurance proposals using computers and solving calculations by hand. I was pretty good at using calculators and even had some experience with computers at that point, which were hard to find other than in college labs. One math aptitude test later, I found myself with a new job, and that's how my journey in the insurance world began.

My introduction to insurance was unconventional, without a doubt. On my first day on the job, my boss handed me a workbook that explained how insurance worked. It included quiz questions that you needed a piece of red cellophane to reveal the answers. The workbook told the story of how, after the death of a breadwinner in a community, often the father of a family, people would pass the hat to help the destitute widow and children survive. Everyone would put in a little, and it would add up to enough to help that one family find their footing again after such a tragic loss. Then, the book covered how creating a formal structure of collecting resources in advance, versus after death, made it easier to provide for people in that situation. Those who had lost someone no longer had to risk waiting for the help and concern of others. *Et voilà*, life insurance was born.

This unique perspective was invaluable. I learned that insurance, at its core, was about pooling resources together to support those in need. This foundational concept was revolutionary for me.

With more research, I discovered that the origin of insurance traces back to the 16th and 17th centuries in England, France, and Holland. The first known life insurance policy was issued in England in 1583, but early insurance groups often failed due to inadequate risk assessment tools. It wasn't until the work of astronomer and mathematician Edmund Halley in 1693—who used mortality tables to calculate life annuities—that the industry gained a more reliable framework. So, comets and life insurance have something in common, after all—save that for your next trivia night!

In Europe, insurance became more established after the Industrial Revolution. However, the situation in America was quite different. Early American colonists faced extreme hardships, such as the devastating "Starving Time" in Jamestown, where starvation and disease claimed almost three out of every four lives. Risks were a part of survival, and if you weren't willing to resort to barbaric things too horrific to mention, then you might not have made it at all. It wasn't until around the 1750s that insurance began to take root in America, gradually evolving into the highly structured and regulated industry we know today.

Specific groups of disenfranchised individuals or those who all worked in the same profession knew that there wasn't a way to care for their families once they passed away. Working in a factory meant risking getting stuck in hazardous machinery or going through some other horrific accident, and if that happened, your family had to face an uncertain future. This scenario was one that others in the same profession, religion, or ethnicity could understand, and they would group together to help their own stay alive and raise children. Initially, people would pass hats around during funeral services to raise money for the widow. Eventually, the system became a little more formal.

Reflecting on my professional journey, I realize how closely it mirrors the evolution of insurance itself—a system that started as an informal way to support each other and grew into a structured, essential industry. The principles of the sharing economy, which emphasize that we are better together, are deeply embedded in the insurance model. If it weren't for humans inherently caring for each other, we'd just resort to kicking aside our weak and letting them die.

A BETTER INVESTMENT THAN SOAP OPERAS

Prior to landing that first insurance company job at the North Atlantic Life Insurance Company of America in 1984, my dad, who worked for the television network, ABC, got me a spot on *All My Children* as an extra. I think I was supposed to drink coffee at a diner during an argument scene between a couple. However, the day they wanted me was the same day I was asked to start at my new job at the life insurance company, so I turned the part down. I would have made $200 that day for a one-time opportunity.

Who knows, I could have been discovered for a coffee commercial down the road? Perhaps the well-known series called *Friends* would have had me as a regular at Central Perk. Or better yet, maybe I could have played Phoebe? *(Smelly cat, smelly cat, what are they feeding you?)*

However, I am not a big risk taker, so I was more attracted to sure bets and a steady income. *(Plus, I was making six digits right off the bat! Unfortunately, two of them were to the right of the decimal point!)* Even a four-figure income was plenty for someone my age back in those days and certainly better than a flash in the pan on a soap opera.

As I kept thinking back to what I learned about the roots of life insurance after first starting my job, I found the history of life insurance to be a fascinating tale of trust, community, and evolving societal needs. Early forms of American life insurance were deeply communal, often born out of necessity. For instance, volunteer firefighters would pass hats around to collect money for the families of their fallen comrades. This act of mutual support laid the groundwork for today's more formalized systems. The Fireman's Fund Insurance Company, founded in San Francisco in 1863, charged a premium of twelve whole dollars so that firefighters could establish a retirement fund for themselves. While this company was not a life insurance company, that fund, and ten percent of the company's profits, went to a firefighter's widow or surviving family upon their death. *(Fun fact: this company helped to fund the Golden Gate Bridge!)*

In the early days, insurance companies often had what we now consider to be quirky names, reflecting their communal origins. Terms like "society" and "benefactors' groups" were common, indicating that these entities were designed for groups of people with a shared bond. Firefighters, religious groups, and farmers were among the first to form such societies. For example, Nationwide was originally created for farmers who resented paying the same auto insurance rates as city dwellers, arguing that rural life posed fewer risks.

One of the earliest and most influential life insurance companies in the United States was the New England Mutual Life Insurance Company, founded by Judge Willard Phillips in 1835. Despite the challenges of raising a guaranty fund during a property bubble, Phillips's reputation for honesty allowed him to secure the necessary funds and write the company's first policy in 1843. This achievement was a significant one, considering it took eight years to convince investors of the venture's merits.

Elizur Wright, a young mathematician, joined New England Mutual in 1844 and brought about significant reforms. His witnessing of an elderly man auctioning his life insurance policy in London, only to see the new policyholder profit from the man's misfortune, deeply affected him. Determined to rectify such injustices, Wright introduced net valuations and non-forfeiture policies, which guaranteed a cash-surrender value to policyholders who could no longer pay their premiums.

The transition from community-based mutual support to a more corporate and transactional model marked a significant shift in the insurance industry. Initially, these groups were tightly-knit, with members sharing a bond that fostered trust and mutual aid. However, as time passed, and frankly some of the common problems got solved, these bonds weakened, and insurance became more of a product than a shared responsibility.

USAA, the insurance company serving military personnel and their families, stands as a modern example of maintaining a strong communal bond. Founded much later than many other insurance companies, USAA thrives because of the tight-knit nature of the military community. This bond ensures a high level of trust and participation among its members, something that many older insurance companies have lost over time.

Despite these changes, the core principle of life insurance remains: it is a collective effort to manage risk and provide financial security. Modern innovations, such as sharing ministries and crowdfunding platforms like GoFundMe, might seem new but are rooted in the same principles which guided early insurance practices. These platforms remind us that the spirit of mutual aid and shared responsibility is still very much alive, even if the methods for doing so have evolved.

This history of life insurance made total sense to me. No preconceived ideas—it was just math and human empathy. This system became an industry, with companies like Prudential *(one of my alma maters)* and others catering to groups of people who did not have systems in place to protect them. Although I initially planned to hold my job at North Atlantic Life temporarily and then return to college, it kept pulling me back in. I did return to school a year later, locally, and my boss convinced me to stay on part-time, which I did. Eventually, I was offered a position with a higher salary when I graduated. *(I made it well into the five figures, before the decimal, by then!)* The rest of my career has been connected to this field as I worked through grad school and up the corporate life insurance carrier ladder.

One thing that has always troubled me about the industry is the lack of appreciation for this ingenious, logical system. Saying you are in the life insurance business doesn't make you popular at parties—in fact, sometimes, the opposite is true.

The industry is known for teaching its agents to "always be selling," often targeting friends and family first. Every social event becomes a selling opportunity, and people can get tired of hearing it. *(See Chapters 9 and 10 to understand this dynamic in a new way.)* With that said, anyone in this business knows there is a huge gap between what the industry generally intends to do and how the public perceives it. This misunderstanding often provokes the sentiment, "Geez, if they only knew…." Witnessing this disparity for myself was the start of my obsession with re-explaining life insurance to a world that has forgotten how and why this system came into being and, more importantly, why it's *different* from other products.

NUANCE 1: Product or Utility?

As an industry, we may have done ourselves a disservice by calling life insurance a "product." A product implies that there is a manufacturer/seller and a buyer. Theoretically, you could have just one buyer of a product and still have an effective transaction. However, the insurance system requires many "buyers" to make it work. The seller isn't really "manufacturing" anything per se; it is pooling resources together to create a contractual arrangement. Without a critical mass of people sharing the risk, there's no product. An interesting note to consider: one of my consulting colleagues astutely pointed out that life insurance is the only product where the consumer is the raw material used to create it! *(I then pointed out that Soylent Green fits into that category as well—ewww! However, it's only fictional, LOL.)*

Insurance, in my humble opinion, more closely resembles a utility in both why and how it was created, as well as how people treat it over time. Think about how you feel about your phone, electric, and sanitation bills, or even about paying for tolls and subways. We get angry sometimes, forgetting that we are all sharing in the cost of these systems. But what's the alternative? Candles? Some people even make it their cause to jump subway turnstiles to protest that subways should be free. Why? Because we are so far away from the origins of these systems that were created for the benefit and sharing of all that we take them for granted. We no longer have any idea how much they cost to maintain, so we don't fully appreciate them. But imagine life without them! I cannot and do not want to. *(Especially the sewer system. Thank you to Strickland Kreass, who invented one of the earliest sewer systems in the US in the mid-1800s!)*

Sharing the cost of these types of systems is a big part of how society makes progress, and as stated earlier, we often take it for granted in the US. But as Bill Gates will tirelessly point out, there are countries in the world that don't have these types of systems built. As a result, children are dying from bacterial infections that result from the lack of clean water, proper sanitation systems, and so forth.

CAN INSURANCE BE FASHIONABLE?

Then, in the last fifteen years, the sharing economy has become fashionable. Technology has enabled people to share all kinds of things—cars, homes, possessions, and even speculations—and therefore making it more attractive than owning the thing yourself. I'm talking about Airbnb, Uber, Lyft, Rent the Runway, and other tech solutions that help people find buyers and sellers for things they want access to but without having to buy them. Sure, these examples are for things that generally make us happier than life insurance does, but the idea of sharing the cost of the solution is the same. Why have a car when you need a ride? Why own a vacation home when all you want is to get away for a little while? Sharing, while an age-old answer among friends, is now possible among strangers, thanks to technology.

The sharing economy, or collaborative consumption, highlights how people can rent or borrow goods instead of owning them and all the subsequent burden. It lets people monetize assets that aren't being fully utilized—like cars, houses, tools, toys, and clothing. In the past, people might have discovered and shared such assets through classified ads or by word of mouth, which would take forever and feel like finding a needle in a haystack. With the Internet and mobile technology, platforms for finding and sharing assets have evolved. These platforms connect people who have underutilized assets with those who need them, making it possible to widely advertise and sell goods and services that used to be provided only by full-time businesses. In the sharing economy, people are both users and providers of resources.

However, defining the sharing economy isn't so straightforward. Some argue that services like Uber and Lyft, which provide rides on demand, aren't truly part of the sharing economy. Instead, they see these providers as part of the gig economy. Meanwhile, platforms like Airbnb, which let people rent out rooms or entire homes, fit more neatly into the sharing economy model. The key is that these platforms facilitate temporary access to goods rather than permanent ownership. *(By the way, I do think it's fair to consider Uber and Lyft as part of both the sharing and gig economy. The cars are being shared, hence the sharing part, and the drivers are getting paid and can do it as a side hustle, hence the gig part. See?)*

And do you know what pisses me off? Insurance is the original sharing model, and we get no credit for it!

That's why I created videos like "The Reverse Lottery" and "The Money Box." These videos are designed to help people understand that insurance is not one-to-one. It's one to many. You either partake, or you don't. When you do, you pay a small amount to hedge the risk of something big and bad happening in the future. When you don't, you take the risk on yourself. Granted, some people may opt for taking on the risk themselves, and there might be reasons for doing so. However, without the understanding of that concept, a consumer may not realize there typically is a choice. These videos aim to help people appreciate—or re-appreciate—the concept of insurance, not be angry at it, lose respect for it, or worse, decide that it's not important.

SCAN ME

Figure 3-4: This QR code directs you to The Reverse Lottery and The Money Box. Scroll down to the "A Sampling of Thought Leadership" section to view these videos."

NUANCE 2: Pennies from Heaven?

I'll never forget the specific event that led me to describe insurance like a reverse lottery. I was doing some research with my colleagues in a facility where focus group participants were gathered. You know, one of those rooms stocked with soda and M&M's, with a two-way mirror where a bunch of people on one side can't see the others. Well, one of the workers there, who was walking in and out, happened to hear me talking about insurance as a pooling concept. The worker was a young man, probably about twenty-two at the time. He said, "Hey, I just wanted you to know I learned something from you about how insurance works. Up till now, I just thought it was 'money from the sky.'"

I thought to myself, "Money from the sky? You ungrateful, little millennial!" But then, I stepped back and realized that he was never told how it really works. Nobody really talks about that anymore. There are hundreds or even thousands of websites that explain how insurance works—i.e. you pay an amount, then get another amount when an event happens—but nobody really explains what makes it "go." This power of pooling is a critical aspect that many people don't understand at all, and if they did, it would make a big difference in their perception of the industry.

I was grateful that he stopped to tell me what he told me. It was a nuance that, if not properly called out as he had, would have gone undetected, an opportunity unrecognized.

His attitude is probably more similar than different from the mindset of the masses today. This skewed understanding of the industry doesn't just lead to insurance professionals being seen as sleazy; it also creates perceptions that can lead to abuses of the system. If people truly think that the money comes from the sky—or they don't really realize it's coming from themselves and their peers—they may look for ways to take more than their fair share. *(Watch to the end of "The Money Box" for a funny depiction of what can happen if I find out someone is doing that.)*

If I accomplish nothing else over my forty-year career, I'd be okay if this concept alone could be recognized and respected. Specifically, I hope you all take a few moments to explain this idea to people, particularly young people, to help them understand. Whether it's students or new people in the business, I believe this lens is the way to get people to truly understand life insurance as opposed to vilifying it. Just like what happened to me when I was young and impressionable, I want other young people to grasp the importance and true intent of life insurance. And better still, it might make insurance people a little more popular at parties.

THE BIG TO-DO

Understand What Makes Life Insurance "Go"

1. **Recognize That Empathy Is a Human Condition:** Empathy is at the core of life insurance. Empathy drives the need for mutual support and shared responsibility in times of crisis. We do not kick our weak aside. Insurance systems are part of how we "de-burdenize" that responsibility of taking care of those who need it.

2. **Recall the Origins of Insurance:** Understand that life insurance was born from communal efforts to support families after the death of a breadwinner. This historical context is crucial for appreciating its true purpose and value.

3. **Remind Peers, Friends, and Young People:** Educate others about the power of many. Life insurance works because it spreads risk across a large group of people, ensuring that the financial burden of loss does not fall on one individual or family. A good opening for such a discussion is when you hear a complaint or someone is looking somehow to cheat the system by taking more from the pool than they really deserve *(or if they think it's "money from the sky")*.

4. **Identify and Address Nuances in Consumer Perceptions:** Recognize that the life insurance industry needs to address the nuances in consumer perceptions and behaviors. Misunderstandings and misconceptions can hinder the industry's efforts to communicate its true intentions. Oftentimes, these nuances are missed by the very people who want change because they use too broad of a brush to gather insights and/or they are not listening deeply enough and with the desire to learn something new. Rather, they might be listening to prove something they already believe. This book comes with a **summary sheet of all the nuances** we will discuss and some explorations to help you get more in tune with them.

5. **Spark Conversations Around Industry Perceptions:** Encourage open discussions about how the life insurance industry is perceived. While solutions may not be immediate, identifying where to look and understanding the areas that need improvement can drive positive change.

CHAPTER TWO

COMPARING DIFFERENT ORGANIZATIONAL FORMS

"Somebody saved me–it happened again /
Somebody saved me–I thank you, my friend."

–PETE TOWNSHEND,
"Somebody Saved Me," 1982

No, we are not going to now have a 101 on the differences between mutuals, stock companies, and fraternals. Instead, we are going to examine intent, which is a subtle, or not so subtle, nuance that serves as a baseline for anything else.

For decades, even centuries, every major–and minor–life insurance company has had its roots somewhere inside a specific group of people who needed a social safety net. Generally speaking, the thrust of creating a system for protecting the destitute came out of necessity. Given what we learned in Chapter One about how human empathy naturally drives us to help those in need, the idea of forming a life insurance company to collect money from many to support the few seems logical and brilliant.

And it is—until we recognize how easy it is to abuse a system like this one. When we start thinking of life insurance as "paying a small amount of money for a larger amount for an unpredictable event in the future," the potential for abuse becomes glaringly obvious. We've all heard many stories, whether made-up or true, about family members who murder other family members for their life insurance. If you're into true crime, life insurance can be a motive that pushes people into doing monstrous acts, corrupting the very thing that is meant to protect families in their time of need.

Of course, there are other reasons why the industry has gained such an unsavory outlook from the general public. Some people have attributed negative personas to the agents who sell life insurance because of a bad experience with one specific person, or they heard a story of someone else's experience but never had one themselves. People on the sales frontlines take the lion's share of the blame, but it often traces further back into the ranks of company executives trying to get sales results and compromising intent to do it. That is why regulations in the United States, and elsewhere, have become so specific, complicated, and, in many opinions, constraining.

I'll admit that I've been guilty of accusing the system of being overly conservative. However, the longer I've been in this business and the more data points I've gathered, the more I appreciate those who have fought against abuse and used the law to protect unassuming people. Since I grew up in New York, the first two life insurance companies *(and the fourth)* I worked for were based there. Behind closed doors, the executives often complained about how difficult it was to do business in New York because the regulations were stricter than in any other state. Companies outside New York often didn't want to do business there at all because of said regulations. But when you look back at the history of the city, the reasoning behind the stricter regulations makes perfect sense.

A great book written in 1907 by Burton J. Hendrick, *The Story of Life Insurance* (Leopold Classic Library), delves into this issue. Hendrick rails against the abuses in the life insurance industry, his timing aligning with the Armstrong Investigation of 1905. This investigation, led by New York State Senator William Armstrong, was triggered by complaints about the practices of executives at the Equitable Life Assurance Society. The bad practices were nothing particularly innovative—just your garden-variety misuse of power and the public's money. However, the fact that they occurred proves that with power comes great responsibility, and without a pristine moral compass, we need laws and punishments for when leaders forget their intended purpose.

In his book, Hendrick argues that there's really no such thing as a dividend in life insurance. More accurately, it's a refund of premiums that were overcharged. He writes:

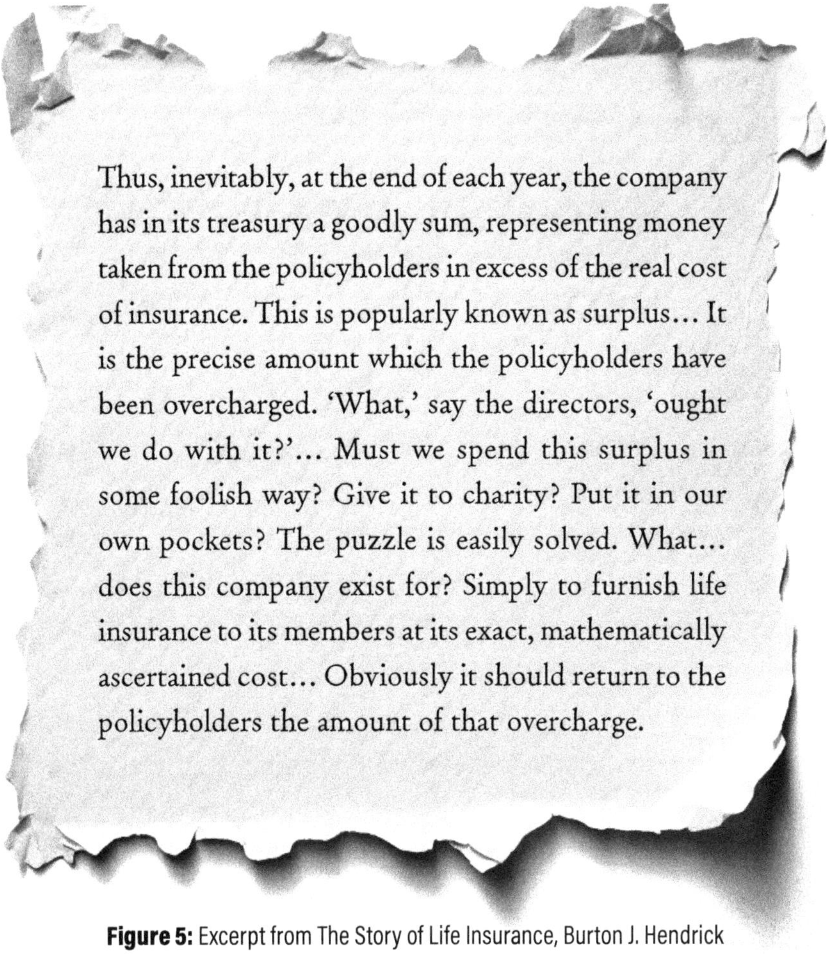

Thus, inevitably, at the end of each year, the company has in its treasury a goodly sum, representing money taken from the policyholders in excess of the real cost of insurance. This is popularly known as surplus... It is the precise amount which the policyholders have been overcharged. 'What,' say the directors, 'ought we do with it?'... Must we spend this surplus in some foolish way? Give it to charity? Put it in our own pockets? The puzzle is easily solved. What... does this company exist for? Simply to furnish life insurance to its members at its exact, mathematically ascertained cost... Obviously it should return to the policyholders the amount of that overcharge.

Figure 5: Excerpt from The Story of Life Insurance, Burton J. Hendrick

The point here is that different forms of insurance companies—whether they be mutual, fraternal, or stock—weren't just random decisions. These forms were created out of some kind necessity. Over time, what started as a necessity became a business opportunity. Now, business opportunities are being pursued within these structures, which, done well, is a good thing. But to truly appreciate the system, we need to understand its roots and remember that its success depends on staying true to the original necessity from which it was created.

"INCAST" VS. OUTCAST: THE ECONOMIC DRIVE TO CREATE FRATERNAL BENEFIT SOCIETIES

Fraternal organizations are a special type of mutual insurance company. Like mutuals, fraternals are owned by their policyholders, meaning there are no stockholders. Additionally, any excess profits are often paid out as dividends to the policyholders. However, fraternals take it a step further—they must give back to their communities in some way, which gives them different, often better, tax benefits than mutuals.

The profits of fraternal organizations must be spent on community initiatives, whether it's organizing walkathons, food drives, or other events. They also have member lodges and branch systems to keep members engaged and involved in governance. Generally speaking, members of fraternals can feel more connected to what's happening within the organization, though there are always variations. Some members are deeply involved, while others barely know their fraternal's purpose—they just bought the policy for the insurance.

The fraternal model appeals to me because it's structured to give back to the community. Unfortunately, many fraternals created decades ago are currently struggling and dying. The communities they defined themselves to serve are shrinking and/or no longer face the same problems that originally led to their formation. As those problems continue to fade, so does the strength of the community bonds they were designed to foster, leading to irrelevance, financial difficulties, and, in some cases, closures or mergers with other fraternals.

There are about fifty fraternals in the United States and Canada. Some are thriving. Many are struggling, as noted above. Some are working hard to reinvent their purpose, grounding it in necessity, so they can be viable into the future. Without that grounding, they'll be just another insurance company with a different obligation, not something special.

So, what is it that unifies people today? How do we reinvigorate these organizations to serve a new purpose?

NUANCE 3: What Problem Does It Solve and for Whom?

The fraternal community can benefit by taking a big step back and looking at today's problems. The reason fraternals thrived in the past was that they solved a specific problem—often related to discrimination or an outsized risk that wasn't being addressed properly. Fraternals require a common bond between their members, which used to be things like religion, occupation, or ethnicity. Back then, if you were, for example, a Catholic, a Lutheran, or of Slavic descent, you were often treated differently, and that commonality brought people together to form fraternals. As society has recognized the flaws in this behavior, the practice has become less common.

Several years ago, I was involved with a deep body of research intended to discover whether or not the concept of a fraternal benefit society is still relevant, and if so, what would need to be done to revive it. What my colleagues and I found is that the inherent idea of a fraternal benefit society is quite attractive, especially for those who are already considering the purchase of life insurance. After all, if people have the chance to buy life insurance from a company that must give its profits back to the community versus giving them to shareholders, with all other things being equal, which do you think consumers would choose? The idea of a fraternal benefit society seemed like a well-kept secret to those who were discovering it through the research process. When people hear the word "fraternal," they think of college frat parties or Fred Flinstone's Water Buffalo Lodge. It makes you think hard about how to make these companies relevant today. *(One way would be to call it something else—aka, stop using the "F" word!)*

A more important way to make fraternals *(or should I say "aternalsfray")* hyper-relevant would be to relook at what bonds people together today. What are the common enemies for key groups of people now? A good thought exercise can start with imagining that these types of companies were never formed and what the world would look like without them. Better yet, pretend that today is the day they were invented. What problems would they solve?

If fraternals were being created today, they might form around issues like managing diabetes, HIV, or transgender health concerns—conditions that affect mortality and morbidity rates and where people feel they're being treated unfairly. Whether or not that's true, the perception of unfair treatment is enough to form a group with a common bond. One that says, "I am part of a group versus excluded from one." Here's where the superpower of the insurance industry—pooling risk—can be once again highly useful. If such groups were to transparently see how their contributions impact the collective whole, there'd be great respect. Hopefully, more people would join. The point isn't just to find and foster a business opportunity but to genuinely solve a problem for a community. If you go into this type of company with the wrong intentions, that is, just for purposes of profiting, people will notice that right away. Then, the effort will be inauthentic and ultimately unsuccessful.

DEATH ISN'T WHAT IT USED TO BE: THE IMPACT OF RISK MITIGATION AND ECONOMIC PROGRESS

Over the past two decades, the field of medicine has witnessed remarkable advancements, particularly in the treatment and management of various diseases. While the goal of curing diseases remains a formidable challenge, there have been significant achievements in eradicating or effectively controlling several life-threatening conditions. These breakthroughs have not only improved survival rates but also enhanced the quality of life for millions of people around the world. Getting some of these diagnoses is no longer necessarily a death sentence. Instead, with treatment, most people can go on to live normal lives.

One of the most groundbreaking achievements in recent medical history is the near-eradication of hepatitis C as a chronic condition. Historically, hepatitis C was a lifelong affliction, leading to severe liver damage, cirrhosis, and even liver cancer. However, the advent of direct-acting antivirals (DAAs) has revolutionized the treatment of this disease. These antiviral medications target the virus directly, disrupting its replication and effectively clearing it from the body. As a result, hepatitis C has transitioned from a persistent, debilitating condition to one that can often be cured with a simple course of medication lasting a few weeks.

Cancer, long considered one of the most formidable enemies of human health, has also seen significant strides in treatment, particularly for certain early-stage cancers. While a universal cure for cancer remains elusive, advancements in early detection, targeted therapies, and immunotherapy have dramatically improved outcomes for specific types of cancer. For instance, early-stage prostate cancer, testicular cancer, and some forms of leukemia, such as chronic myelogenous leukemia (CML), can now be effectively treated, especially with early intervention. Targeted therapies, which focus on specific genetic mutations within cancer cells, have shown great promise in treating these conditions.

Likewise, the story of HIV is one of the most remarkable in the history of medicine. Once considered a death sentence, HIV has been transformed into a manageable chronic condition thanks to advances in antiretroviral therapy (ART). While a complete cure for HIV has not yet been achieved, there have been cases of functional cures, particularly in patients undergoing bone marrow transplants for other conditions, such as the famous "Berlin Patient."

What does that mean for life insurance companies? It means the demographics have changed. Instead of death lurking at every corner, people can now consider ways to cure their conditions or live with them—and that is why some companies are considering how best to serve these individuals.

It could also mean that it's time to look at what changed about society and identify where the disenfranchised might be. We see more and more people who might have different lifestyle choices, hobbies, or other beliefs forming community bonds together. These factors, along with several others, now contribute to new ideas for using the insurance industry's superpower for new and different groups.

I recently learned of an example of a new kind of bond when I discovered a new Insurtech—a term used to describe new tech companies that focus on insurance—startup (www.insuredbylotus.com), that is focusing on the problem of infertility. Apparently, one in five couples will be diagnosed with infertility, and many Gen Z people are concerned about this finding. This case is a great example of a new kind of common bond.

WHEN PROFIT ENTERS AS A MOTIVE

Stock companies are owned by shareholders, which means they have a responsibility to generate profit for those shareholders. After all, shareholders made the investment, and they expect a return for it. Plus, they give these companies an easier way to raise capital for the sake of growth. But when you layer a profit motive on top of something like life insurance, which is supposed to be about sharing risk and providing financial security, it feels "crowded." Life insurance, by its very nature, seems better suited to focus on covering the true cost of loss *(as astutely explained above by Burton Hendrick in the early 1900s)* rather than generating excess profit.

In addition, we have seen the emergence of start-up companies occupying some narrow space in the insurance arena over the last decade or so. While these companies are not typically publicly traded, they are backed by investors who often are looking first for returns. Founders often have a passion for solving some kind of problem in the industry by using better technology. And because starting a new venture is difficult in and of itself, the motivation often shifts from that of solving the identified problem to gaining financial traction to stay in business until critical mass is hit. In other words, it transforms from a passion to serve to the need for survival. While this shift is completely understandable, it typically doesn't work unless the problem being solved is defined properly, quantified as being important enough for a large group of people to solve, and the solution truly works. It also really helps if investors have patience because they, too, are passionate about solving the problem.

I have no qualms with profit-making in general, but in this context, focusing first on generating profit feels at odds with the goal of mitigating the cost of risk. Some companies that were mutuals and went public in the 90s and early 2000s are now exiting the life insurance business because it's not profitable enough. However, if the primary goal was to provide financial security to policyholders, shouldn't the focus be on fixing the business model to make it sustainable first and foremost?

NUANCE 4: Profitable Enough?

If you want to solve problems by pooling together people's money, solve the problem and make enough money to keep things running well and to keep the highly talented people who are adding value motivated to keep doing so. While the movie character we know as Gordon Gecko may have stated very famously that "greed is good," and that may be true for Wall Street, it really isn't true for an industry where people are sharing financial risk and using each other's money as their shields. While being profitable enough–as opposed to operating near a loss–is a prudent cushion in case there's a math mistake or unforeseen set of events *(which is what surplus is for)*, where's the room for "excess?" Some would ask, "Where's the line?" I say that if you have to ask, you may have already crossed it. It's not about an amount of profit, it's about why you need to have it in the first place. Is it the main motivation, or is it the outcome of doing a better than anticipated job of running the business and predicting claims?

Another profit-motivated concept that particularly irks me *(as it did Elizur Wright in the 1840s)* is the concept of life settlements, where a stranger can buy your life insurance policy if you decide you no longer need it. They give you money for it and then keep the policy in place, waiting for you to die so they can collect the death benefit. It's perfectly legal, but it doesn't sit right with me. Imagine someone betting and hoping that your life expectancy is shorter than the insurance company predicted for the sake of a nice profit–there's something deeply unsettling about that. *(Life settlements are unsettling? LOL.)* I know life settlements serve a purpose for those who really do need money now and are willing to forego the death benefit to get it; however, there are other ways this goal could be accomplished so that the "stranger-danger" isn't part of it.

These statements are not meant to argue against capitalism or support socialism. It is fair for people to earn money when they create value. If others are willing to pay for that value, then the creator of it deserves profit. However, in the life insurance business, what people are paying for *is* money. Future money. They pay an amount now in the form of premiums for a larger amount later when it matters most. While factors like customer service and brand are part of the package, excess profits mean that people may be paying more than necessary for the sole purpose of someone else taking it. If prices have to rise to support these profits, then customers are either overpaying *(which they will likely not do in the presence of other choices)*, or companies may have to leave the market because they can't compete.

So, let's sum everything up by saying it's not fair to compare corporate forms of life insurance as much as it's not as fair to compare corporate forms of life insurance companies as it is to compare their primary intent. Then again, we don't really know what that is, and we often use the corporate form of the company to make judgments about it.

THE BIG TO-DO

Remember the Why

At the end of the day, it's crucial to remember why life insurance was created in the first place. It wasn't about profit—it was about necessity. Can we remember our roots and focus on providing real value to people, addressing genuine needs, and ensuring that the noble purpose is upheld? By doing so, we can maintain the integrity of the system and continue to provide the financial security that so many people depend on.

1. **Evaluate Current Business Practices:** Assess whether the life insurance companies you're familiar with or work for are staying true to the principles of sharing and necessity. Are they focusing more on profit or on solving real problems for policyholders? You can tell by what people are talking about, spending their time solving, and what is keeping them up at night.

2. **Identify Modern Needs:** Think about what issues or challenges today could be the common problem for specific groups of people. Are there underserved communities facing specific risks that could benefit from a shared insurance model? If we say we want to exclude people within certain types of risks, consider what would be possible if these risks are analyzed and viewed with an eye toward the future state, where these risks are likely to be better mitigated than they are today. A current ex-

ample would be programs that leverage the tracking of health metrics that can dynamically change prices *(as pioneered by John Hancock and Vitality)*. Taking this concept a step further, how might the anticipation of improving medicines or other discoveries change how these risks are viewed and priced? What looks like yesterday's "no" might be tomorrow's "yes."

3. **Seek to Understand:** Data is abundant today. When disenfranchised groups in the past formed their own insurance pools, it's because they felt they knew something about the risk that others didn't, even if they were wrong. What might that look like in these current areas?

With an eye toward the why, there may be new ways to consider these modern challenges without making them fit into the box that the industry has already created.

CHAPTER THREE

CATEGORICAL UNFAIRNESS

"One of these things is not like the others / One of these things just doesn't belong / Can you tell which thing is not the like others?"

–SESAME STREET,

"One of These Things (Is Not Like the Others)", 1969

Let's talk about our need for categories. You know, our tendency to categorize everything in life so that we can wrap our heads around it? From how we organize the books in a library to how we create a wedding guest list, categories make life easier for us to navigate. And, yes, that applies to products, too–especially when it comes to understanding why some things fly off the shelves and others sit there collecting dust. And, wouldn't you know it, life insurance lands in one of those tricky categories that require a little more effort to get moving when it comes to demand. It's what we call "sold, not bought." **This phrase is the crux of what I mean by an unfair comparison.** Let me explain.

Economics 101 teaches us that demand is what drives people to buy products or services. However, not all demand is created equal. Different types of demand depend on the product being sold and the overall market. In very simple terms, consumer demand fuels production, stimulates economic growth, and contributes to lower inflation and interest rates. The demand for a product tends to heavily contribute to the price of the thing you are trying to sell. Let's take a look at a few examples of different types of demand, to see where life insurance fits into this picture.

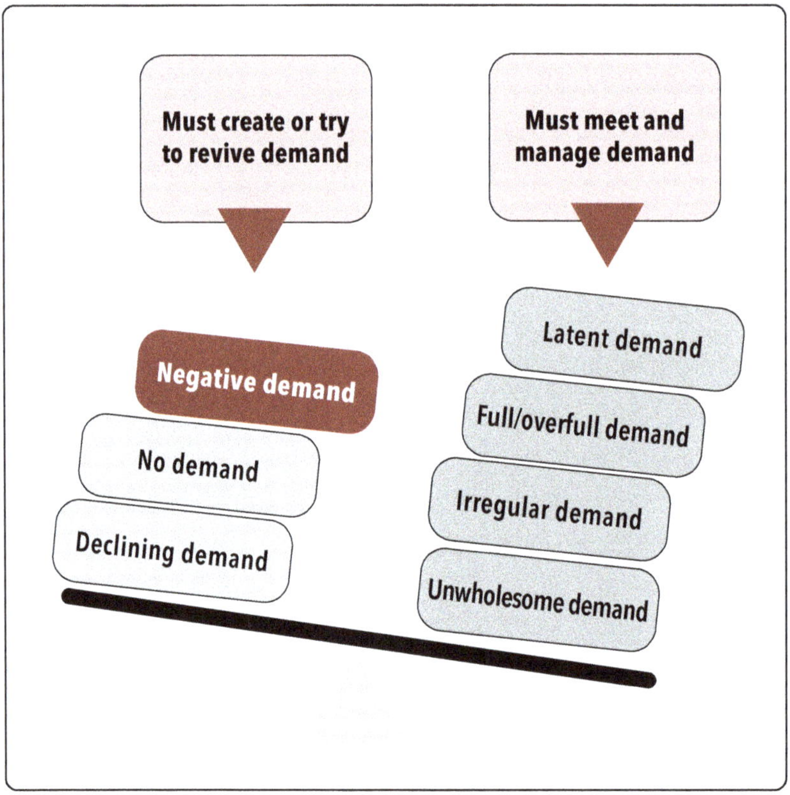

Figure 6: Different Types of Demand

We've got **full demand**, when people want plenty of something, and it's available everywhere. Think Coca-Cola, shoes, or even the latest iPhone. These are things that people want, and they can easily get them through any of the normal channels. There's no need to convince anyone to buy, as people are already willing and able to do so. That's the dream, right? The product practically sells itself. You wake up and think, "I need milk, I need sandwich ingredients, I need gas for my car." You don't need to see a commercial to sell you on any of these things—other than which brand you choose, perhaps. The regular weekly checklist of items at the grocery store falls into this category.

Then, there's **unwholesome demand**—the stuff people crave but probably shouldn't. We're talking about things like illegal drugs or even fast food. Cigarettes and alcohol also fall into this category. Demand is high, but it's not exactly good for us to use these products. Because of that, the supply is often hidden or irregular. You want it but might have to go through a few hoops to get it. There also tends to be more rules and regulations to deal with because people's health might be at stake.

Next up is **overfull demand**. This one's fun—imagine the toy your kid desperately wants for Christmas. It hits the shelves, and boom, it's gone. Every parent in town is scrambling to get their hands on it, and Santa's having a little crisis because there just aren't enough toys to go around. So, what do you do? You hop on eBay and pay ten times the price just to make your kid's holiday magical. That's overfull demand—people want it so badly that the supply can't keep up, and they're willing to overspend, if necessary, to gain access to it. *(Thank you, Taylor Swift.)*

NUANCE 5: Need Does Not Equal Demand

But then, there's negative demand. That is where life insurance comes into play. Negative demand doesn't mean that there isn't any need for the product. In fact, it's often something people know they need, but they actively avoid getting it. This example is one of the most important nuances, and unfair comparisons, in this book. The industry has done a great job of quantifying the number of households that do and do not have life insurance. In fact, a 2024 study by LIMRA and Life Happens finds that over 102 million people do not have a life insurance policy. However, in this case, need does not equal demand. Demand must be cultivated.

Think about dental procedures, for example. No one wakes up excited to get their teeth cleaned or, heaven forbid, a root canal. But you know it's something you have to do, even if you'd rather not think about it. Life insurance is the same way—it's necessary, but it's not something you seek to buy. In fact, people will go out of their way to avoid it until something or someone forces them to confront the need. *(In the case of the root canal, it's typically severe pain!)*

That's the reason life insurance is often labeled a "sold, not bought" product. It's not like the latest gadget or fashion trend that people are lining up to buy. It's something that requires a nudge—whether it's from an agent, a life event, or even a close call that makes someone realize, "Hey, I really need to prepare in case I'm not so lucky next time." That's where the challenge lies for those working in the industry. It's not just selling a product; it's selling the idea that planning for the future, especially the not-so-pleasant parts of it, is worth doing right now, not later. *(My first book helped professionals to understand the unpleasant parts and make them less so. It's called Flirting with the Uninterested!)*

WICKED PROBLEMS

A helpful distinction that I learned about from working with my colleagues at Maddock Douglas is a term called the "wicked problem." Getting the life insurance protection gap closed is an example of a wicked problem. Not wicked in the sense of evil, but wicked in the sense that problems like this one are very complex. The variables are always changing, and oftentimes, the attempts to solve them result in making the problem worse on some level. This terminology was put into use in the 1970s in the area of social policy making. One of the common denominators of a wicked problem is that they involve human behavioral change on some level, which, as we know, is very challenging. *(Think of "quit smoking" and "no more drunk driving" campaigns, or even bans on sugary sodas, etc.)*

In the context of innovation, wicked problems can be contrasted with "tame" problems, which also can be complex, such as building a skyscraper or a bridge. However, tame problems, once solved, can be applied anywhere, again and again. That's because the solution always follows a similar pattern. The conditions for solving it are predictable. Wicked problems don't have predictable patterns. They must be chipped away at, with solutions evolving and iterating over time, and are not necessarily replicable everywhere with any certainty that they'll work.

The tangled ball of yarn or wire image that you see below is often used as a metaphor for a wicked problem. If you attempt to untangle it on one side of the ball, you may create a tighter tangle on the other end. That's why solutions to wicked problems have many facets, and you must put things into action on a small scale to know if they will work. I'll give you an example of such a "tighter tangle" inside of a wicked problem that you can relate to.

Figure 7: Wicked Problem is a term used in social policy making, and often involves human behavior change.

Think about what the life insurance industry did in the 90s. The cost of insurance rates (COIs) were reduced to make products more competitive. Multiple preferred classes were created, which made it cheaper for some, more expensive for others. It added more complexity to the sale and made it harder to earn a living selling life insurance. It also made the underwriting process much more complex and hard to automate. I'm not suggesting this decision was a mistake necessarily, but it was handled with an engineering mindset instead of a human-centered design mindset. Not all of the potential consequences were considered, and it may have actually contributed to the life insurance protection gap.

Is the problem wicked or tame? This question is another distinction of what makes for a fairer comparison. Are you comparing the life insurance industry to another industry that is dealing with a wicked problem, too? If not, reconsider.

DEMAND CREATION: NOT FOR THE FAINT OF HEART

Now, let's talk about what it takes to actually get people to take action in this category. It's not for the faint of heart, that's for sure. When you're selling something that people don't really want to think about, you're up against human nature itself. We're wired to avoid discomfort, and what's more uncomfortable than thinking about death? Exactly. So, it's no surprise that selling life insurance often feels like pushing a boulder uphill. You have to approach someone, often someone you don't know very well, and ask, "Hey, when was the last time you thought about dying?" Well, you may not ask that, but it sure might feel like you're saying that.

There are also other human complexities that are involved beyond just thinking about death. That's the obvious one. But when mastering nuances, we must go beyond the obvious.

When someone is "nudging" you to make a decision that you know on some level you need to make *(such as eating healthier, moving more, drinking less alcohol, quitting gambling, etc.)*, people often feel judged or deprived in some way. They may not verbalize that feeling, but it's there. Guilt may also come into play as well, because if these decisions are not made or are put off, it can feel like we are hurting someone else. *(More on judgment, guilt, and shame later. How fun!)* Anger might also come into play as well. In one research study I was involved in, observers were surprised to hear one man verbalize his feelings about having a lump sum of money available to his family after his death, angered by the idea that they might be living a better life without him than with him. He was especially upset at the thought that his wife may live it with someone else. That's dark, deep, and real.

As much as we'd love for life insurance to be a product people just buy because it's a smart and responsible decision, the reality is that most people need to be convinced to take action. Think about kids who don't want to go to the doctor or adults who don't want to take out the trash. To be accountable for convincing them to do so? Well, much like parenting, it can take a lot out of you. It's not just about explaining the benefits and the value of life insurance—it's about overcoming resistance, fear, anger, and sometimes outright denial.

That's why those of us in the business have to be resilient. We have to be willing to engage in difficult conversations and be prepared for rejection. And not just a little rejection, either—sometimes, it feels like rejection is around every corner. However, when you finally get through to someone and help them see the importance of planning for their family's future, it makes all the effort worth it. You're not just selling a policy; you're providing peace of mind, and more importantly, security for others. That's something people might not realize they need until you help them see it.

Think of the benefits that you're helping people to realize. When you feel the "commission breath" on you, or you feel yourself panicking because you haven't met your sales goals, remember, that's not the point of selling life insurance. The point is to help people mitigate the risk. You are, in a modern sense, passing the hat around for widows and children, but doing it before the terrible event, not after the fact. At least this way, nobody has to wait around forever for the financial gap to be covered, or worse, rely on generosity of others at a time when there's already so much stress.

Death is a frightening, overwhelming, and emotionally charged certainty in life. But what isn't certain is when it will happen. When someone understands the level of risk and how it might affect their loved ones, then they might begin to understand your "why" that drives you to reach out. In order to better convey that "why," you need to believe it first and genuinely make it the reason for selling life insurance.

As a marketer with a textbook education *(which, by the way, doesn't hold much value in a negative demand category)*, I learned about two basic types of marketing: push and pull. This lesson is Marketing 101. Push marketing focuses on incentivizing every layer of the distribution chain to sell a product, while pull marketing starts with the consumer. It creates a message or campaign that makes people say, "I want that."

Pull marketing is the sexy, glamorous side of the industry. It's the kind of marketing where someone comes up with a genius campaign that takes the world by storm, leading to iconic catchphrases like "Have it your way," "It's the real thing," "Just do it," or "Where's the beef?" These campaigns leave a lasting impression in the minds of consumers, go on to win awards, and mark their creators as being advertising geniuses. However, in our industry, push marketing is the dominant approach, and typically "genius" is not used to describe those efforts.

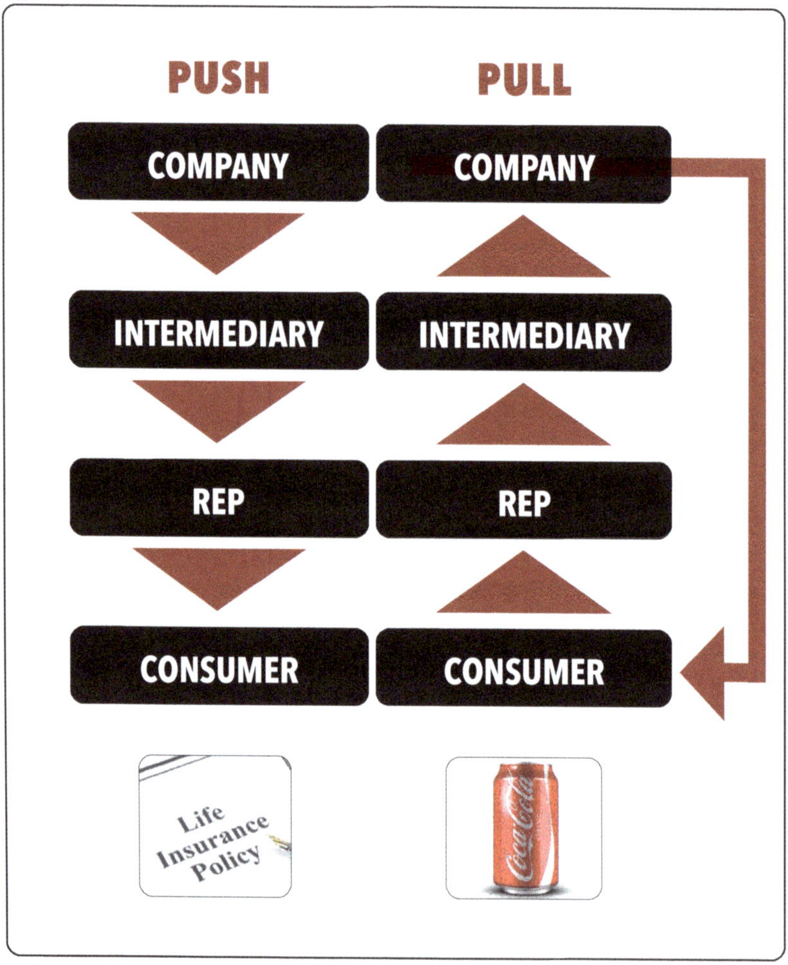

Figure 8: Push Marketing vs Pull Marketing

That fact is due to the nature of our industry. Honestly, we do a pretty good job with what we have. If we didn't, we wouldn't be here.

DE-SHAMING THE COMMISSION MODEL

Speaking of selling, let's talk about the elephant in the room–the commission model. If there's one thing that makes people wary of life insurance agents, it's the idea that they are motivated by huge commissions. Growing up in the 1980s and 1990s, we were bombarded with stereotypes of sleazy salespeople, not to mention pyramid get-rich-quick schemes. That type of imagery sticks with you, and it's no wonder that people might be a little hesitant when an insurance agent comes knocking or calling.

When you buy life insurance, you're contributing to a system that helps families when they need it most. The commission model, when done ethically, is simply a way to incentivize agents to spread this important social safety net–and to put up with all those emotional dynamics of the "sold, not bought" category. It's not about making a quick sale; it's about ensuring that as many people as possible have the protection they need.

That's why it's so important to understand how the commission model came to be. Sure, there will always be bad apples in any industry, but for the most part, life insurance agents are in this business because they believe in what they're doing. They want to help people, and they deserve to be compensated for their efforts and willingness to fight the human tendency to resist or avoid these topics.

Given that it is often difficult to get people to take action, the commission being much higher in year one *(anywhere from 50% to a 100% of the premium paid could be typical)* makes sense. The initial sale is where a lot of the effort, discomfort, and drama is. Agents and advisors invest time, effort, and patience into every sale. They deal with getting dragged along, ghosted, maybe even hung up on. Not to mention the complexities of dealing with carriers who are typically not known for elegant and easy processes. Furthermore, the sale itself might be finished when the customer purchases a plan, but that doesn't mean the agent is finished. Agents will have to maintain relationships with their contacts, clients, and other sources throughout the years, re-convincing them to keep the valuable insurance they purchased. Speaking of which, it's why it still makes sense to have renewal income from the sale of life insurance.

NUANCE 6: Commission as a Percentage of What?

Now, is it perfect? Nothing is. There are unintended consequences of these structures, but the basic idea is not shameful. One thing to consider *(and it is kinda weird, I admit)* is that life insurance commissions are typically a function of the premium paid for it, not the amount of insurance bought. So, it's akin to a real estate agent getting paid as a percentage of your mortgage payment versus the price of the house.

Here's a scenario that someone could use to de-shame the commission model.

Two guys walk into a bar. They are both forty and in good health. One is considering buying a home, for which he will need a $500,000 mortgage loan at 7% for thirty years at a fixed rate, which will be about $3,300/month without taxes or fees. The other is considering buying a whole life policy for $500,000, which is about $700/month or $8,400/year in premiums. The commission to the real estate agent is 6% on the $640,000 price of the house, or $38,400. The insurance agent will receive 80% commission on the first year premium and then a much lower yearly amount after that. **The two men share their upcoming plans and note how the real estate agent will make a 6% commission and the insurance agent will make an 80% commission.** However, in the first year, the real estate agent will earn $38,400. The insurance agent will earn $6,720. Over a thirty-year period, the agent might receive an additional $13,000 of commission on that sale if the policy stays in place. Which of the two gentlemen is getting a better deal? The answer? **This comparison is unfair and irrelevant!** But it's useful in demonstrating that 80% is not a high number when you consider what it's 80% of! Yet, people make blanket statements about how high life insurance commissions are just because there's no real understanding of what it's grounded in.

TAX BENEFITS: A SPOONFUL OF SUGAR

"Just a spoonful of sugar helps the medicine go down / In a most delightful way!"

–MARY POPPINS,
"A Spoonful of Sugar," 1964

Now, let's talk about one of the things that can make life insurance a little more appealing—the tax benefits. Life insurance offers a range of tax advantages that can sweeten the deal for buyers. From tax-free death benefits to tax-deferred growth in permanent policies, these benefits are designed to encourage people to plan for the future and protect their families. Who doesn't like a little extra incentive when it comes to making financial decisions?

Permanent life insurance can build cash value, giving you a financial cushion you can tap into while you're still alive. This money could help you supplement your retirement income, cover medical expenses, or act as a safety net in emergencies. The best part? The cash value grows tax-deferred, meaning you won't owe income taxes as long as the funds stay within your policy.

You can withdraw up to the amount you've paid in premiums without paying taxes. If you take out more than that, you'll owe income tax on the amount above what you've contributed. There's another option, however, which is borrowing against your cash value. If you take a loan instead of withdrawing, you won't owe any taxes on the gains you borrow.

This strategy can help the insured stay in a lower tax bracket during retirement and avoid taxes on Social Security benefits. The loan doesn't need to be repaid while they're alive; if they pass away with a balance, their death benefit will cover it, with the remaining funds going to heirs tax-free. However, keep in mind that the insurer will charge interest on the loan. If the loan and interest end up being more than your total cash value, you'll need to make additional payments or risk the policy lapsing. You can take out cash value lines of credit with the policy as collateral to avoid this risk to the policy. Then, when there is a death, the outstanding balance can be paid off with the proceeds.

The whole point of this information is not to sell you, the reader, on the tax benefits of life insurance, but rather to help you understand how they can be enticing to those who understand and use them as intended.

But with any tax benefit, there's always the risk of abuse. Unfortunately, there are always going to be people who try to game the system. Some folks in the industry have found ways to exploit these benefits, creating complex tax schemes that push the boundaries of what's within the spirit of the laws. When that happens, it leads to tighter regulations and increased scrutiny of the industry as a whole, which can threaten the very benefits that make life insurance attractive in the first place. So, overselling a spoonful of sugar has its drawbacks.

In the 80s and 90s, various tax-driven schemes were sold to everyday people. Interest rates were high, and policies looked very attractive as an alternative to pension plans, promising to provide retirement income in a "more efficient way" than a traditional one. The problem was that the numbers didn't add up because the assumptions didn't hold up. If the policy couldn't sustain over time, the entire plan fell apart. For the tax benefits to remain, the policy had to stay in effect until death. When that didn't happen, the tax benefits were lost, triggering tax liabilities or the need to pay more than they thought they had to. Worse yet, many of these everyday people didn't realize they bought life insurance. They thought they bought a security plan or investment. The legal and regulatory communities responded with much stricter rules around these kinds of sales and redefined the circumstances under which one is allowed—more like not allowed—to compare life insurance to investments.

Ultimately, it was clear that these schemes were a form of sales abuse. Once a lawyer got involved, a class action lawsuit was filed, resulting in large settlements paid by insurers. Afterward, it wasn't just one company—it spread to the next company and the next, as they were all engaging in similar practices.

Risky tax schemes are not just bad for the consumer. They are bad for companies themselves and further pollute the integrity of the insurance pool, driving costs upward for all.

So, when we remember the origins of these benefits and understand them in the context they were meant to be used, it can keep us on the right path.

SERVING THE UNDERSERVED: THE MIDDLE MARKET DILEMMA

"Standing in the doorway thinking of the past /
Making plans tomorrow hoping it would last /
From the wrong direction, you can lose your way."

–THE HOFFMAN BROTHERS,
"The Best Is Floating By," 2022

Tax benefits are intended to incentivize everybody to purchase life insurance to protect their families; however, the attractiveness tends to skew toward wealthier people who have even more incentive to reduce taxes. As a result, one of the biggest challenges we face in the life insurance industry is ensuring we're serving everyone, not just the wealthy. There's a tendency for advisors to focus on high-net-worth clients because that's where the big money is. When you're trying to make a living on commissions, it's tempting to go after the clients who can afford the largest policies. The unfortunate consequence often means that middle-income families are left unprotected or under protected.

Growing up in a middle-class family, I understand how important financial planning is, even when money is tight. For many middle-income families, life insurance feels like a luxury they can't afford. They may not see the value in it, or they may feel like they're not "worthy" of professional financial advice. This belief creates a gap in the market, where the people who need the most help are the least likely to get it.

We have been talking about this issue for a long time now as an industry. It's time to think differently about it. One of the things we hear repeatedly in common industry research is that the middle market can be served through automation, making it easier to purchase. But that assumption has not panned out for reasons we will discuss later. Now, there's a "back to the future" soundbyte going around that talks about the fact that we do, in fact, need a person in the mix. While I agree with this point, it's not for the same reason that's being surmised by this "pendulumesque" thinking.

As we think about the human desire to try and make things easier on ourselves, you can see why leading with tax benefits is a natural tendency. This inclination explains why sales to the wealthy are not only attractive to the agent, but also why there may be more inherent motivation for the client to take action, thereby reducing resistance and friction the agent may face.

Speaking of other human tendencies, there's another category dynamic that's really important for us to talk about here, and that is the role of fear that runs both deep and complex.

HUMAN RESISTANCE: THE ROLE OF FEAR

In the negative demand category, selling often feels like you're pushing a rope. It requires convincing, nudging, and sometimes even pulling people across the line. At the heart of all this resistance is fear—fear in the minds of the agents and advisors selling it, and fear in the hearts of the clients resisting it. Understanding this fear is crucial to understanding why the life insurance industry operates the way it does and why, despite all the technological advances and digital innovations available nowadays, the role of the agent remains indispensable.

Figure 9: Image from an old life insurance ad leveraging the fear of death resulting in your children becoming orphaned.

Back in the day, the tactics for selling life insurance were pretty straightforward—and a little heavy-handed, to be fair. There was a technique known as "backing up the hearse," where the imagery used in advertisements was designed to shock people into action. Think 1940s print ads showing crying babies and distraught widows after the death of the family's breadwinner. The fear of loss, of leaving your loved ones destitute, was the hook that reeled people in. It worked back then, partly because advertising wasn't as transparent as it is today. People weren't as savvy to the tactics being used, and the emotional pull of such imagery was strong.

Fast forward to now, and things are a bit different. We live in an age where consumers are more aware, more discerning, and frankly, more skeptical of anything that feels the slightest bit manipulative, even if it's ultimately for their own good. Here's another important factor: women are playing a much bigger role in financial decision-making than they did in the past. In fact, they are dominating these decisions as a whole. Women tend to be natural worriers, already wired to think about the "what ifs" in life. So, using fear as a sales tactic often backfires. You pile on more fear, and you're likely to push people further away rather than pulling them in.

For a new agent entering the business, it's a double whammy. They have the fear of the consumer as described above, but they also have the fear of being seen as that outdated, pushy salesperson who nobody wants to associate with. This worry is often labeled a "fear of rejection," but it's even more than that. What does rejection mean? Being disliked? Not accepted? Alone? Isolated? These are terrifying human fears and are difficult to overcome. **Training protocols have not addressed this concern of being overly pushy, and if anything, may even have doubled down on the levers that were pulled in the past for purposes of cultivating sales.** All too often I have seen people enter this profession with hopes of being successful, and then, when they find out what they are "supposed to do" to get clients, they run away.

So, how do you create demand in a category where there is naturally little to no demand and now has more savvy consumers who can smell sales tactics a mile away? How do you avoid being seen as *that* person? That's the million-dollar question, and unfortunately, there isn't a simple answer. Over the years, various strategies have been tried, but many of them miss the mark because they fail to account for the nuances of human behavior and the deep-rooted fears that drive it. But there's hope.

It seems that everyone wants something from you—your time, your money, your attention, your love. That's a big part of why selling life insurance can feel so thankless. It's not just about convincing people to part with their money for something they can't benefit from today; it's about convincing them to confront their own mortality to plan for a future they'd rather not think about. Therefore, the role of the agent isn't going away anytime soon. Digital platforms and AI can help with efficiency by streamlining certain parts of the process, but they can't replace the human touch needed to navigate these emotionally charged decisions. The **non-logical** pieces of the equation, such as the fears and doubts people have surrounding death and what happens to their loved ones afterward, require a real person on the other end of the conversation—someone who can build trust and guide clients through the process.

A MICRO NUANCE

When mainstream research reiterates the importance of the human touch, this is why. It's not just because of transactional complexity, it's because of the complexity of being human. Most research subjects can't articulate that. It's something that must be observed from multiple angles and thousands of data points. It's easy to attribute the success—or lack thereof—of our industry based on things that people say, but it's harder and more important to do it based on what people feel and will do.

What are people afraid of? My research over the years has proven that it's more than just thinking about death. It's also the fear of being "duped" by someone else—i.e. buying something you "don't need," or worse, finding out by someone you respect that you got duped, bought the wrong thing, paid too much, etc. It's such a tangled web of emotions and all things illogical but yet extremely human and a very strong driver of behavior.

UNDERSTANDING FEAR: A DEEP DIVE INTO THE HUMAN BRAIN

To really get to the heart of why selling life insurance can feel so difficult, we need to look at fear from a biological and psychological perspective. Coach, author, and consultant Steven D'Annunzio spoke with me on the different elements that come into play when agents are reaching out to prospective customers.

He said:

> There are two pathways of fear in the brain. I'm talking about Pathway 1, which involves the more primitive parts of the brain: the reptilian brain and the mammalian brain. The reptilian brain is more basic, while the mammalian brain, which includes the amygdala and limbic system (or midbrain), is slightly more advanced. When stress hormones are triggered in the mammalian brain, which is still part of the brain's system, you experience a strong fight-or-flight response. You might feel an intense urge to escape the situation or even lash out physically.

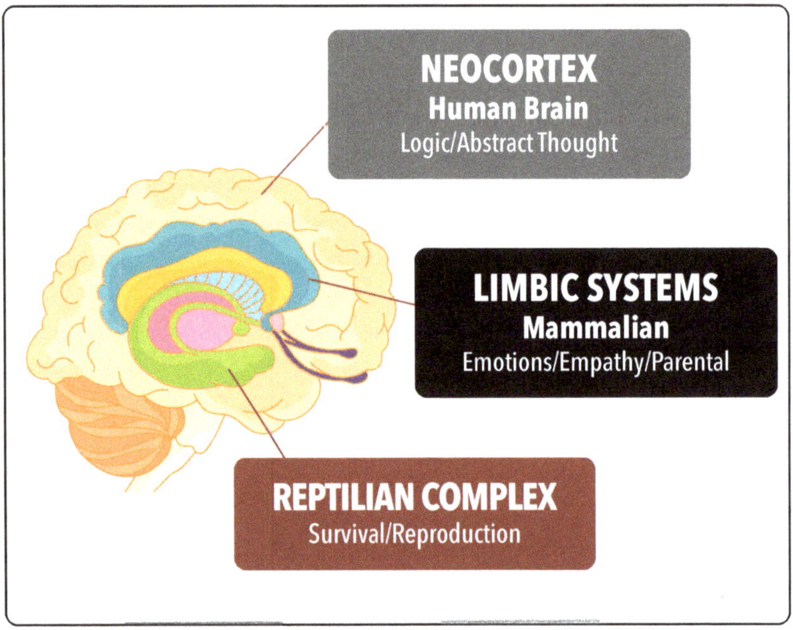

Figure 10: Map of the human brain

NUANCE 7: Physical and Emotional Threats Can Trigger the Same Behavior

The trouble is that our brains can't always distinguish between a physical threat and an emotional one. So, when a client is faced with a conversation about life insurance—which forces them to think about death, financial insecurity, and the unknown, or even become concerned that this stranger may be violating their personal space, stealing their time, or using them for their own personal gain—their amygdala lights up just like it would in a dangerous situation. Stress hormones start flowing, and suddenly, that conversation feels like something to avoid at all costs. It's no wonder so many people push back (fight), make excuses (flight), or say they're "all set" (flight).

Overcoming this level of stress is where the challenge lies for advisors. You're not just selling a product—you're trying to overcome a deeply ingrained biological response. When people are afraid, they aren't thinking with the logical part of their brain. They're not weighing the pros and cons of a life insurance policy; they're just trying to get out of an uncomfortable situation.

TRANSCENDING FEAR: FROM SELLING TO SERVING

Steve D'Annunzio also told me:

> When I conduct workshops, one of the key things I emphasize is the importance of personal experience. I always tell participants, "Don't just take my word for it—trust your own experience." One of the main areas we focus on is managing fear. I use a tool I call APRIL, which stands for Awareness, Presence, Releasing, Intention, and Love. The idea is to move beyond fear by cultivating a higher mindset, shifting from fear to love. And by love, I don't mean it as an emotion, but as a way of influencing brain chemistry—actively working with your brain to face your fears and set intentions to do good for others.
>
> When you do so, you're transitioning from selling to serving, from a mindset of scarcity to one of potential prosperity and abundance. It's like football: the team that blocks and tackles better will win. In the financial services profession—whether it's life insurance, equities, disability, long-term care, annuities, or other financial contracts—the equivalent of blocking and tackling is prospecting and gathering referrals.

The challenge we face is twofold. First, there's managing our own fears, and second, there's reaching out to enough people with a trustworthy offer. We also need to move beyond what we've traditionally been taught in our profession, such as relying solely on the fact-finder approach. Instead, we should focus on what I call the "feeling finder." This term means understanding what's happening emotionally with the person we're contacting and finding a pathway to build trust with them.

Another thought leader I admire in this space is Raeanne Lacatena. She is someone I was introduced to by Steve D'Annunzio and who has coached me one-on-one. In her new book, *The Integrated Entrepreneur*, she talks about a method she developed to transform fear into productive behaviors:

It is called STEAR, Clear and Anchor. It starts with using the STEAR method, and then clearing negative thoughts and anchoring on positive ones.

The STEAR Method is a practical critical-thinking tool that helps us organize our thoughts and create new relationships with whatever is happening in our lives. The method involves breaking down your current reality into its various components, including the facts, thoughts, emotions, actions, and potential results. By doing so, we can identify any negative or unproductive thoughts and emotions and reframe them into more useful and positive ones.

The "S" stands for the situation—the facts about the event that lead you to want to process your current set of circumstances. These are just the facts of what's going on right now.

The "T" stands for thought(s)–what thoughts or beliefs are coming up when you think about what you are going through. In this step, we explore all the thoughts that aren't very useful, loving, or productive. This could include thoughts about yourself, others, events, your past, present, future, or anything else that your mind tries to tell you about the facts of what is going on right now.

The "E" stands for emotion(s)–all the emotions and feelings that come up when you think about those not-so-useful or less than-loving thoughts. Let yourself explore how it feels to think those thoughts.

The "A" is for action(s)–all the actions that tend to come, have already come, or might come as a result of leaning into those negative or non-useful thoughts or feelings. How would you behave or how have you already behaved because of the way you are thinking and feeling about the event?

The "R" stands for result(s)–imagine the results that could come from engaging those thoughts, feelings, and actions that are not very helpful. If you continue down this road, what could happen?

Clearing and anchoring are techniques that can be used to help us release and shift any negative or unproductive thoughts and emotions that we may be holding onto. Clearing involves acknowledging and releasing negative thoughts and emotions from our body and mind, while anchoring involves creating a positive and productive physical, emotional and mental state to reinforce those changes. When we combine these two practices, we can create a powerful tool to support us in moving forward with our desired outcomes.

We are combining formal thought-work, personal development, neuroscience, and some higher-fuel practices, such as spiritual practices or energy work, to fire on all cylinders, change that internal programming, get to the root cause, and create a completely new relationship with that root in order to create completely new patterns, thoughts, emotions, behaviors, and results in our lives.

For more information on this method, visit theintegratedentrepreneur.com/STEAR

There's a universe of tools that are now emerging to help humans navigate the complex process of...well...being human! In the past, philosophies and tools like these may have been seen as purely spiritual and not scientific enough to be scalable and credible. Not so much anymore.

I've often said it's hard to be a human and then try to find concrete solutions for changing human behavior. If we could hire Vulcans *(you know, from the well-documented planet Vulcan, home of Mr. Spock from Star Trek)* to assess us and give us the report, we'd probably be in a better position to make change. But until we discover intelligent life forms on other planets, learn their language, align on common values, and then offer them consulting jobs, we are stuck with us ordinary folk to feel our way through it.

I applaud the thought leaders like Steve and Raeanne in this space who are making strides to mainstream these tools and techniques. Not just for the purpose of being more effective at selling something like life insurance, but for navigating the complexities of a rapidly changing world where fear and anxiety are now dominant. This problem is real, and the pressure will continue to intensify.

If You Think Selling Life Insurance Is Hard, Try Selling People on the Idea of Doing That for a Living!

While it takes a certain type of person and with a specific mindset to be good at this profession, it takes an even higher level of passion to bring the *(many needed)* people into this business.

My husband, Jim, happens to be one of the people who has done this task successfully for almost his entire career. He's seen successes, failures, surprises, disappointments, turnarounds, and happy accidents. One thing is for certain: when you've seen one story, you've seen *one* story. Everyone is different. Yes, there are patterns we can learn from. However, until you are fully inside the other person's head and learn who they are, what they love, and what they are afraid of, you don't know what's driving their successes or failures.

THE BIG TO-DO

Shifting from Sales Tactics to Fear Management

At the end of the day, doing this job is about more than just selling policies. It's about helping people protect their families, plan for the future, and find peace of mind. To succeed in this industry, we need to shift our focus from traditional sales tactics to managing fears—both our own and those of our clients.

What does that mean from a practical perspective?

1. **Help agents understand the difference between this category** and others, anchoring on why people feel the way they feel.

2. **Examine how we are currently training agents to sell**. How well does it line up with the way current day consumers view sales tactics? Specifically, reaching out to their closest one hundred friends and family and asking for an opportunity to talk with them about their finances. This idea is terrifying for most people. Instead of starting here, what if we focused on the management of fear first? If we did nothing other than that, would the outcome be different?

3. **How would you do it? The few techniques referenced here might be a start, but there's more where that came from.** This opportunity is a chance to pull a new lever.

We can't change the fact that life insurance is a "sold, not bought" product, but we can change the way we approach it. By understanding the unique challenges of the category and addressing the fears that hold people back, we can create demand in a market that is naturally resistant. It's not easy, but it's worth it. After all, we're not just selling insurance—we're helping people secure their futures, and that's something to be proud of.

CHAPTER FOUR

THE TWO-WAY EXCHANGE

"Is there anybody out there?"

–ROGER WATERS/PINK FLOYD,

"Is There Anybody Out There," 1979

How many marketing emails, texts, and snail mail solicitations do you receive every day? How many of them try to appear as though the person is talking to you, but you know that it was likely sent to many other people as well? These are examples of what I would call "one-way" exchanges. One person or entity wants to engage with another; however, the other party either doesn't know about it, may not care, and may not even want to engage. In fact, the person or entity initiating the exchange often doesn't know who they are attempting to engage with, either. *(This book is a one-way exchange!)*

Conversely, a two-way exchange is when both parties are aware and agree to the exchange. An important nuance I have learned over decades of experience is that in a "sold, not bought" category, no sale is ever made without a two-way exchange happening beforehand. So, the questions are: what is a two-way exchange, and how does it happen?

First off, a two-way exchange is any exchange of information between two humans *(well, I guess pets can be involved, but that's not relevant here)*. It's is a conversation that could be in the same room, over a phone, video call, text, chat, or email, or any other way you can think of. The other party knows who they are specifically talking to. It is in contrast to the one-way communication, which could be a blast email where the blaster doesn't know who is reading it until they respond, and the receiver probably knows the email wasn't meant for them alone.

Every sales conversation in life insurance starts with some kind of two-way exchange. You might be thinking, "That's not true, Maria. People buy insurance online all the time without having any conversations about it." That notion appears to be true; however, when you really look at those instances, you'll find that there was some kind of initial conversation that sparked the purchase. Granted, it may not have been with a salesperson or an agent. A discussion could have been had with just about anyone.

On a daily basis, we're interacting with several people, having conversations spanning multiple topics and serving multiple purposes. We converse with family members, friends, neighbors, co-workers, people we might see at school or church, or someone we run into at the market. Each one of these conversations has the power to sway us into thinking about a topic, which in turn might influence us into purchasing something to alleviate a concern of ours or solve a problem we've been having. Not every two-way exchange is a sales conversation, but every successful life insurance sales conversation *must* start with a two-way exchange.

TWO-WAY EXCHANGES CAN CREATE DEMAND IN A NEGATIVE DEMAND CATEGORY

A two-way exchange prompts another person to recognize a need of theirs and to take action. In the context of life insurance, it involves engaging someone in a meaningful dialogue that imparts the importance of buying life insurance and how a specific company can best fit the need.

As stated earlier, this interaction can take many forms, and not just in a professional setting. It can occur with a friend, family member, a stranger you just met, or a TikTok influencer. The key element is that this exchange happens in real-time and involves authentic, reciprocal communication between both parties.

Sales pitches, cold leads, and emails are *not* two-way exchanges until someone answers. Investopedia writes that cold calls are only successful 2% of the time. In my personal and professional experience, I believe that's a generous estimation. According to a 2020 study done by Maddock Douglas, cold leads are now just about dead.

Email marketing is also losing its effectiveness because we're all overwhelmed by the sheer number of emails we receive on a daily basis. Intuit Mailchimp found that in November of 2023, more than twenty-six *billion* emails were sent on its platform. That means most email blasts probably ended up buried, unopened, or in the promotions tab in consumers' Gmail accounts. On the other hand, if someone was already in a two-way exchange prior to receiving the email and considered making the decision to purchase, they may then respond because it was a relevant message at the right time. But let's face it: consumers know when an email is really meant for them versus just trying to sound like it is. *(Case in point, on my birthday, I always get an email from my dentist that wishes me a happy birthday. However, if I were to visit or call the office that day, it would be unlikely that anyone would know that it's my birthday.)*

THE TWO-WAY EXCHANGE IN ACTION

A major life insurance company recently ran an ad that sits rent-free in my mind. The commercial depicts a conversation between a husband and wife.

The wife asks the husband, "Did you hear what happened to Bill?"

"The marathon runner?" the husband responds.

"Not anymore," she says.

Eventually, they get to the part where it is evident that Bill has died. The husband goes, "Are we about to have the '*we need life insurance*' conversation?"

The wife replies, "No, we're about to get the plan." They then get the plan. End of commercial.

That's a two-way exchange. Poorly acted, it may be, but it's an exchange nonetheless. The sales agent didn't initiate that exchange. The fictitious event of the wife having a conversation with Bill's widow was a two-way exchange, and then, the couple had one as well.

Does this exchange *have* to be in person? Of course not. Consider a scenario where two friends are texting each other. One friend asks, "What are you up to?"

The other replies, "Just dealing with some family issues. My uncle passed away." The first friend expresses condolences, which leads the second friend to reflect on the uncle's financial situation and maybe even the importance of life insurance and to eventually decide to buy it. This interaction, despite being virtual, is a two-way exchange because it involves immediate, back-and-forth communication.

Remember, a two-way exchange has two key elements: (relative) immediacy and reciprocity. Unlike one-way exchanges, where information is sent out without an expectation of a response, two-way exchanges involve active participation from both parties. This immediacy is crucial in building trust and demonstrating relevance, which will then prompt action from clients.

THE IMPERATIVES OF A TWO-WAY EXCHANGE

Empathy, individuality (personalization), and authenticity are pivotal in making two-way exchanges effective. Advisors must genuinely understand and address their clients' unique challenges and concerns if any sale is ever to happen. Authenticity builds trust, making the exchange more impactful and increasing the likelihood of a positive outcome. Without authenticity, even the most well-intentioned advice can fall flat and fail to resonate with the client. And worse, it can damage trust.

NUANCE 8: Naysayers Could Be People Who Have Not Had a Two-Way Exchange

Several years ago, at Maddock Douglas, we completed a study to find out more about those who labeled themselves as "not interested" in life insurance. These were the hard doubters, the people who said no to every call and every email they received. For a nominal incentive fee, these naysayers agreed to sit down with our researchers and answer some questions for our benefit, so we could learn more about how they viewed our industry. The researchers were not trying to sell life insurance, but they were genuinely interested in understanding the participants' viewpoints surrounding the topic.

The interviews involved a series of questions designed to explore the participants' reasons for their skepticism. The researcher would ask, "Why don't you have life insurance?"

The participant might respond, "I don't think I need it. My kids are grown up." The researcher would then delve deeper, asking about the participants' past experiences and specific concerns.

As the conversation progressed, some participants began to reconsider their stance. They started to see the value of life insurance and expressed intentions to explore it further. They'd say something like, "You know, I guess I should probably start thinking about life insurance policies. I will probably look into it."

We were watching from behind the glass and jumping for joy as if we had made a scientific breakthrough. It wasn't an agent, a family member, or some terrible life crisis that prompted them to make that discovery. They had come to that realization on their own during a conversation with a complete stranger. What was keeping them in the seat was the initial fee of about $150 for their participation. Otherwise, they would have never sat still long enough to listen or think about insurance as a viable option for them.

The researchers didn't push or pressure the participants; they simply listened and engaged in a meaningful dialogue. The intention of the conversation wasn't to change their minds, just to understand their viewpoints. This approach can be incredibly effective in overcoming skepticism and prompting action from potential clients. We had an "Aha!" moment all together, realizing that there had to be someone to just listen to the clients' thoughts and concerns in order to flip them from being disinterested to actively engaged in the conversation.

Now, obviously, we can't regularly pay people to sit and listen to us or engage in a thought-provoking conversation with a disinterested third party. *(Or can we? Hmmm...)* However, there can be ways to spark positive thoughts about life insurance and get others to realize that they might need it at some point in their lives.

So, to reframe this issue of what creates demand, I'd say there are two critical elements: **a two-way exchange and an attention span.**

REAL-TIME COMMUNICATION, AUTHENTICITY, AND MEANINGFUL RELATIONSHIPS

In the past, insurance agents would go door-to-door to visit prospective clients and existing clients with policies. *(For those born after 1990, this practice is called the debit system, and although it still exists, it's largely gone away.)* They would have been welcomed by the homeowners, who would invite them in to listen to what they had to offer, and more likely than not, the two parties would have been friends. Cups of coffee would have been poured, and perhaps even freshly baked cookies would have been offered.

These days, no one wants visitors in their home, especially visitors they may not know or trust. The COVID-19 pandemic only solidified that shift. If you don't believe me, watch stand-up comedian Sebastian Manascalco's hilarious routine about this shift. He describes his childhood and how when the doorbell rang, and he didn't know who it was, his mom would answer with glee and break out the Entenmann's cake because they had "company." But now, if the doorbell rings and we don't know who is there, we tell our families to turn off the lights, hit the floor, and grab a weapon. What makes us laugh about his joke is that there's a lot of truth to it.

Since those kinds of visits are usually no longer a viable option, phone calls may seem like the perfect solution, but calling clients can also have some issues. Phone calls can be too much emotional labor for most people, who are burned out from work, caring for their families and friends, or just living their daily lives.

Yet, the two-way exchange still rings true despite all these other changes in the world. How can an agent understand the power and purpose of the two-way exchange? *(By the way, three-way, four-way, five-way, etc., exchanges all are great options, too, as long as every party knows the others are involved and that they are not just considered a name or number.)*

A WORD ON CONTEMPORARY METHODS OF ENGAGEMENT

For younger generations, contemporary methods such as online chatbots, social media interactions, and live streams can facilitate two-way exchanges. Platforms like TikTok, which offer live streaming and interactive features, provide opportunities for real-time engagement. These platforms enable people to connect in a manner that feels personal and immediate.

Most people under the age of forty understand the concept of parasocial relationships with influencers. For those unfamiliar with the term, it's what happens commonly with celebrities. A fan may extend interest, energy, and time to that celebrity, who doesn't even know they exist.

Influencers might discuss problems that come up in their lives and share them with an audience, who might then take those conversations and convey them to family members. The web of two-way exchanges creates a domino effect that will lead more people to a website, phone number, or platform. Grassroots sources are more appealing than ever, and our study predicts their influence will spread. By 2023, the wisdom of the crowd predicted that most consumers (70%) will look to nonprofessionals for advice. And this prediction, my friends, is happening right now. ***(LOL, see what I did just now? I called you my friend, but I really don't know who is reading this book.)***

On TikTok, for instance, someone can host a live stream where they discuss the benefits of a product or idea and answer viewers' questions in real time. This act not only educates the audience, but also builds a sense of community and trust between the influencer and their followers. Similarly, on platforms like Reddit, influencers can participate in "Ask Me Anything" sessions, where they engage with users in a direct and interactive manner.

Can advisors create engaging and relatable educational content, knowing that consumers find it as valuable as the product itself? *(I know the compliance world is cringing right now, but we must consider these dynamics as part of the future, even if they are restricted today.)*

NUANCE 9: When Non-Professionals Say It's Good, It's Magical

Over the last year, I saw something I never thought was possible. Influencers on TikTok are making a big deal about cash value life insurance *(referred to as Infinite Banking, a term coined decades ago by Nelson Nash)*. My husband, Jim *(who, as mentioned earlier, is also in this industry)*, and I began getting questions from millennials and Gen Z asking about the concept and if it was legit. Digging further, we found out where they heard about it and helped them understand it. For the first time ever, life insurance became organically cool! It's important to note, however, that the person/people who are promoting on TikTok are not agents. They are influencers. If they were agents, they would have had significant compliance violations for lack of disclosure. However, conceptually, these influencers are not wrong, and people got it. And even better, they are engaging with it! Eureka! These all qualify as two-way exchanges with humans, even though there's technology between them. What can we, as an industry, learn from this instance and do with it?

Despite its many champions, artificial intelligence hasn't reached the level of being able to talk about irrational, illogical concepts such as fears, moods, concerns, desires, choices, and recommendations. Consumers want to know that their risks are being mitigated and that someone on the other end of the line cares about whether or not they get the best option for their situation. An agent can make recommendations based on a situation that an AI chatbot just cannot do. There is innate comfort in hearing, "I've been in *(or worked with people)* in your shoes, and based on my experience, this option is the best one for you." That is the power of the two-way exchange. Chat GPT, on the other hand, will present all the balanced facts and come just short of suggesting what to do with them. This statement is not a criticism of AI; it's a lesson in expectation management. Should AI make recommendations? If it did, would you trust them? Hmmm.

THE IMPORTANCE OF SOFT SKILLS

Developing soft skills, such as empathy and active listening, is essential for advisors. These skills help advisors understand their clients' needs and build trust with them. Clients prefer advisors who listen to their concerns and provide tailored advice rather than those who focus on the merits of the products they are selling.

Empathy involves putting oneself in the clients' shoes and understanding their feelings and perspectives. Active listening means fully concentrating, understanding, responding, and remembering what the clients say. These skills are critical in establishing meaningful connections and fostering a sense of trust and reliability between the two parties.

Just as authenticity (being real) creates powerful, successful two-way exchanges, inauthenticity has the power to completely turn off a prospect. If someone gets the sense that they are being sold something, or if at any moment the interaction feels forced, or in someone else's best interests, they will shut it all down. Unfortunately, consumers are especially sensitive to upselling "pushes" in the current environment. Approaching clients with anything less than a genuine willingness to help is a major turnoff to them, therefore making meaningful two-way exchanges impossible.

NUANCE 10: The Invisible Wall

To shed more light on the impact of authenticity, I'd like to introduce a concept I call the "Invisible Wall." For context, let's look at the customer experience cycle according to Dubberly and Evanson. There are five phases.

- **Connect and Attract:** how you get people interested
- **Orient:** how you set expectations for what the customers' experience will be like
- **Transact:** where the deal is sealed
- **Extend and Retain:** where other services and products might be provided
- **Advocate:** where the clients are supposed to tell everyone how great it was *(BTW, this stage doesn't happen too much in a negative demand category, even when the experience is awesome, unless otherwise prompted.)*

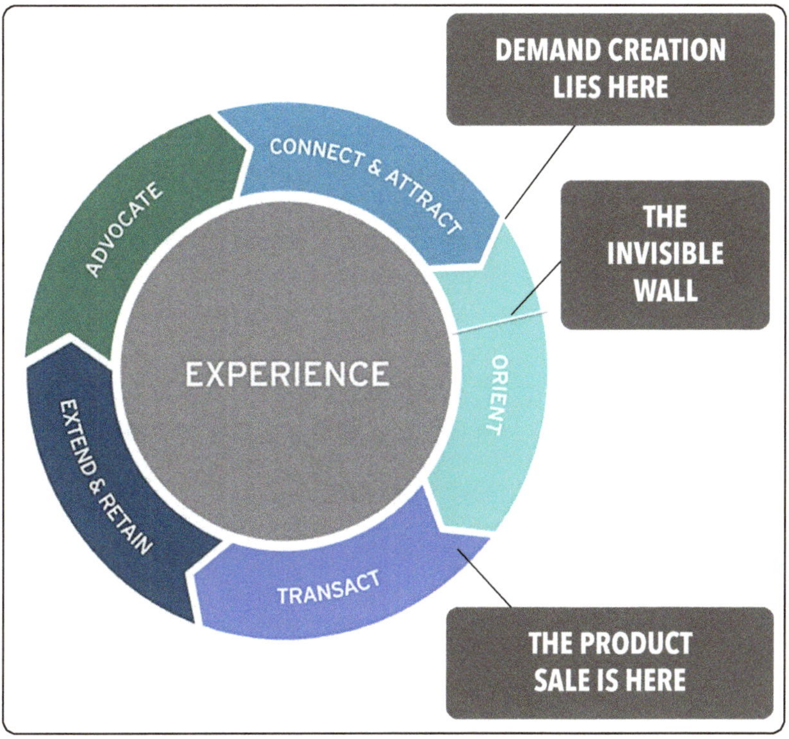

Figure 11: The Customer Experience Cycle according to Dubberly and Evanson

What we have been focusing on for many, many years is how to improve the transact phase of the cycle, the product sale. I applaud the industry for making tremendous strides in this area. We can now do it in minutes! *(Or so I am told. I involved my team in a mystery shopping experiment with several platforms, and some performed in that regard. Others didn't.)*

However, the transact phase is not what creates demand. Demand creation lies somewhere in the often undernourished orient phase.

At a straight angle, the wall doesn't look like much. But if you turn it on its side, you see how big of an obstacle it really is. It's like an invisible wall that stands between the average person whose family would benefit from having life insurance and the decision to acquire it. The wall is filled with their fears and concerns, preconceived notions about where their money is going, and assumptions that they won't need life insurance at all, or worse, someone might judge them for what they do or do not purchase.

Figure 12: Exposing the "Invisible Wall"

Most of our industry's tech work is directed at keeping the experience great for those who have already flipped over the wall. *(Harkening back to the concept of wicked versus tame problems, once someone flips over the wall, the problem becomes more tame.)* It is a small, relative number that everyone is competing for in the online space. Digital platforms often assume that making the purchase process easy will suffice in getting consumers interested in obtaining policies. **That is flawed thinking and likely at the crux of why many digital darlings of Insurtech have failed.** The challenge lies in getting people to recognize the need and take action at all.

THE JUDO FLIP OVER THE WALL

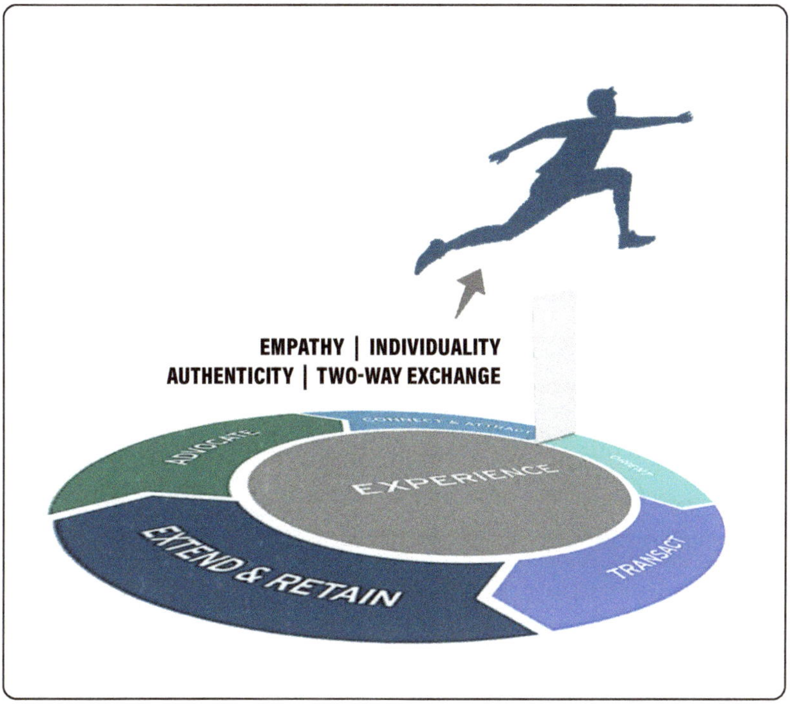

Figure 13: Getting people over the Invisible Wall

Two-way exchanges act as the ladder to help individuals "flip" over this invisible wall. Through meaningful interactions, advisors can nudge clients towards recognizing the importance of life insurance and deciding to buy policies. This process involves listening, displaying empathy, and utilizing authentic communication. When the message suddenly comes together for them, they flip from undecided to "Okay, I'll do it." Flipping someone over that wall doesn't typically happen on the first try. Rather, it takes a nurturing individual to keep checking in with a prospective client over the course of a few months. If you get a hard "no means no," then it's over for now, but not necessarily forever. Just keep in mind that if you've established a genuine connection with this person, then it might be worth resurrecting that exchange once more when enough time has passed.

By maintaining this ongoing exchange, the advisor builds trust and keeps the conversation open. Over time, as the clients' circumstances change, they may become more receptive to the idea of purchasing life insurance.

Timing is crucial in these interactions; however, the circumstances that create good or bad timing are out of the advisor's control. Advisors, therefore, must follow up at appropriate intervals and give more information about the good things that come with a new policy. Incentives, such as highlighting tax benefits or investment values, can also help motivate individuals to take action. The real key is being there at that moment when the person is finally ready, versus giving up too early.

THE COMMON MISCONCEPTION ABOUT THE FLIP

The problem with focusing all of one's marketing energy and crafting platforms for those who have already made the flip is that there aren't enough "flippers" out there to justify the investment. Digital platforms and advisors often compete fiercely for these individuals, assuming that the number of flippers is larger than it actually is. Many an Insurtech investor pitch has been made using the large numbers of those with need, not the small numbers of people who are already ready to buy.

Startups that build on the idea that need equals demand will run out of quality leads over a relatively short time. The lack of interest will inevitably cause those companies to either go out of business or pivot to a new approach. You cannot successfully create demand without a genuine two-way exchange. *(Plus, there's also showing empathy, listening, and all the other actions that go into understanding and caring about the person's concerns and desires.)*

THE CHALLENGES OF DEMAND CREATION

The cost of creating demand through advertising and messaging is high, and achieving scale in converting flippers into buyers is challenging without meaningful human interaction. For instance, digital platforms might invest heavily in online ads, assuming that these will generate immediate sales. However, without two-way exchanges, many potential clients may not feel compelled to take action without first talking to an actual person who can answer their questions or ease their concerns, even if that person is not a professional. Oftentimes, this action is taken "off the grid," especially when the other party is not a professional, meaning that the company who sponsors the platform has no visibility into it. The real value lies in the combination of digital tools and personal interaction.

Consumers want to be seen, heard, and known by advisors they trust. And once they are in a relationship of trust with an advisor, they may likely ask for advice on other topics as well. In fact, the 2020 study by Maddock Douglas on the post-pandemic future of the trusted advisor predicted that consumers will look to a smaller number of professionals to serve more of their needs in the future, often outside of the advisors' core service areas. Advisors who make the effort to deepen relationships with existing clients will reap the rewards. This prediction is definitely playing out in the real world today.

So, the real question is, "Can the two-way exchange be scaled?" The flip comes less from what we say we will deliver and more from how long we can keep someone's *attention.*

Given the current state of robotics and AI, let's assume that a meaningful, two-way exchange about a complicated subject is still a human responsibility. If you can accept that for the moment, let's then talk about our expectations relative to scaling.

How Do You Keep Up with the Joneses? (And the Smiths, and the Davidsons?)

You might be thinking, "But, Maria, how on Earth am I supposed to form authentic connections with all these people?" After all, the human mind is limited by its ability to maintain meaningful relationships. If you don't believe there are limits, ask anthropologist Robin Dunbar.

Figure 14: Understanding Dunbar's Number

"Dunbar's Number" suggests that humans can recognize up to 1,500 people's faces, have 500 acquaintances, maintain meaningful relationships with about 150 people at any given time, have fifty friends, fifteen good friends, and five true loved ones. This ratio was determined through studies involving neuroimaging and observing time spent on grooming within communities of apes, which is a crucial social behavior among primates. Dunbar concluded that the relative size of the neocortex–the brain region associated with higher-order functions like cognition and language–correlates with the size of an effective social group. This ratio essentially defines the complexity that a social system can manage. What I love about the Dunbar concept is that it shows you the limits of the human brain. You can only maintain so many meaningful human connections without becoming overloaded or without sounding inauthentic. And inauthenticity is a death sentence for anyone making a living as an advisor.

If you bounce around those numbers, this concept aligns with the 10-3-1 ratio used in the life insurance industry. Each number goes down the line by about a third. This information sure is compelling.

THE 10-3-1 RATIO

The 10-3-1 ratio, developed by Al Granum in the 1970s, is based on the idea that for every ten people an advisor contacts, three will agree to a meeting where there is a meaningful exchange of information, and one will eventually buy life insurance. This ratio has held steady over the years and highlights the importance of persistent, targeted efforts in building a client base.

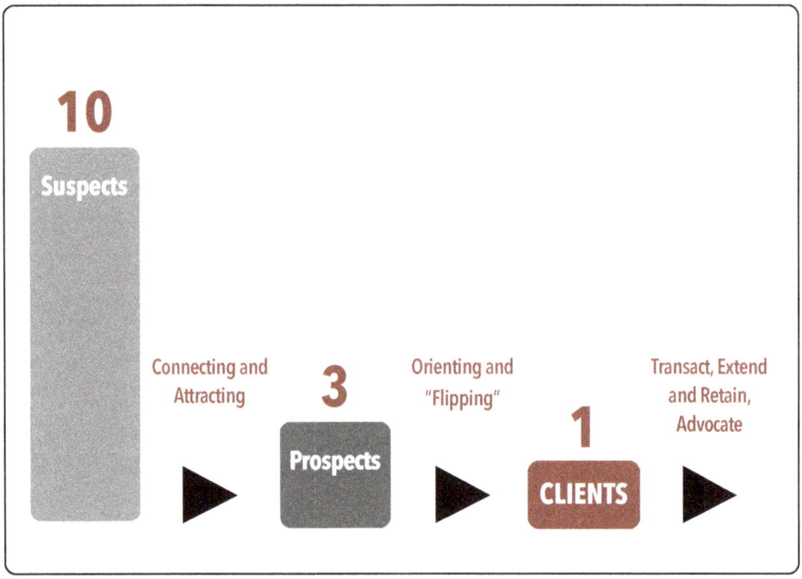

Figure 15: Al Granum's 10:3:1 Ratio

While Granum may never have been exposed to the work of Robin Dunbar, Granum deeply understood the value of the two-way exchange and must have instinctively known that there are human patterns to be learned and mastered. He once told an interviewer, "The best way to get someone to listen is through a referred lead. I could spend all the time in the world mastering a magnificent presentation, but I still need someone to talk to. It was on that basis that I put my foot down."

Granum instructed agents to meticulously document referred leads, noting details such as cases opened, closed, and business submitted. This data was recorded manually, as computers weren't yet available for these tasks. In the initial ten years, they successfully maintained accurate records for over 50,000 referred leads. Their research indicated that out of every ten leads processed ("suspects"), three would become prospects, and one of those would convert into a client. Further analysis of data collected over the subsequent fifteen years on 150,000 leads confirmed the 10-3-1 ratio. Notably, *this ratio remained consistent regardless of the agent's level of experience.*

IMPROVING THE RATIO

Executives in the life insurance industry have become obsessed with the idea of "beating" these numbers. Why not 10-5-2, after all? That would double our success rate. Many attempts were made to give people better sales tactics, objection handling, and closing language. However, if we stop and align this goal with Dunbar's recognition of the limits of the human brain, it's easy to see why the ratio always holds. It's less about what the agent may be saying and more about how tired their brains get of retaining information on people who didn't say yes, all while finding new leads. With limited brain capacity to hold meaningful exchanges, someone's gotta go. And who knows, those people might have said yes with just one more call. So, the answer still is to leverage human brains. But with more thought given to how teams of humans, plus technology, could retain more meaningful relationships, I am not giving up hope that the ratio could improve. There's more to be learned by the next nuance.

NUANCE 11: It Takes a Village

While team-based selling is not a new concept, I believe that it can be reimagined into more than just selling. With teams of people with different skills, clients could be acquired, served, and serviced. There's an old-style model in the legal profession called the Finder, Grinder, Binder, Minder model. Finders perform really well at interacting with clients. They know how to open doors and are great at introducing people. They are people-oriented. They get the party started.

Grinders figure out what the problem is and how to solve it. They are exquisitely nerdy and smart, but not necessarily social. Often, they act behind the scenes. So, it's hard for them to make money from commission-based business models unless they attach themselves to Finders.

Binders close the deal. They ask for the check. They are not afraid to hear "no." They will give tough love and challenge those who can't commit to something so important because of fear. But they, too, must also possess soft skills; otherwise, they might be off-putting.

The Minders? They forget nothing. They know all the to dos, the follow ups, and the outstanding items. Plus, they respond in a caring, nurturing way like nobody else could. They make sure the ongoing issues are resolved, even after the commission is earned and spent. With the help of AI, we could perhaps speed up the signals that would clue the humans in on the right time to do something, making this role even more efficient.

While these four roles might be played by less than four people, the distinctions are important. Do we have the best of each skillset working together for the betterment of a client? If the answer is no, why not?

If you're tempted to say "we do that" or "we tried that," consider this argument. If you are doing it and it works, can you replicate it? If you failed, do you know exactly why? If it's related to the reluctance to share commissions, have you considered fear as the possible root cause and dealt with that effectively? If the answer to these is no, you may have missed a nuance or two. Closer examination and tracking of data are key.

THE BIG TO-DO

Be More Patient When Doing Observation for Valuable Insights

The key takeaway here is the importance of two-way exchanges in life insurance. We must recognize the need for meaningful, empathetic conversations and continually refine their soft skills. While technology can assist in the process, the human element remains crucial in building trust with and fostering positive action from clients.

However, the bigger question is, "How did we overlook this important nuance of the creation of demand and spend billions on technology that assumed the demand was already there?" Here are some thoughts about how to avoid that mistake in the future:

1. **Patient Observation:** Professionals wanting to make an impact here should focus on patient observation. This step is simple, but not easy. Too often, observers lose patience, miss important nuances when listening for clues, and move on too quickly. They don't read between the lines enough and ask "why" something is true. There's a great tool used for innovation and design thinking called Problem Statement Laddering, or simply

"The Five Whys." As you observe those whose behavior you understand, try asking "why" something is true. When you get the answer, ask "why" again. Once you've asked it up to five times, you will likely discover something new that you were not aware of before.

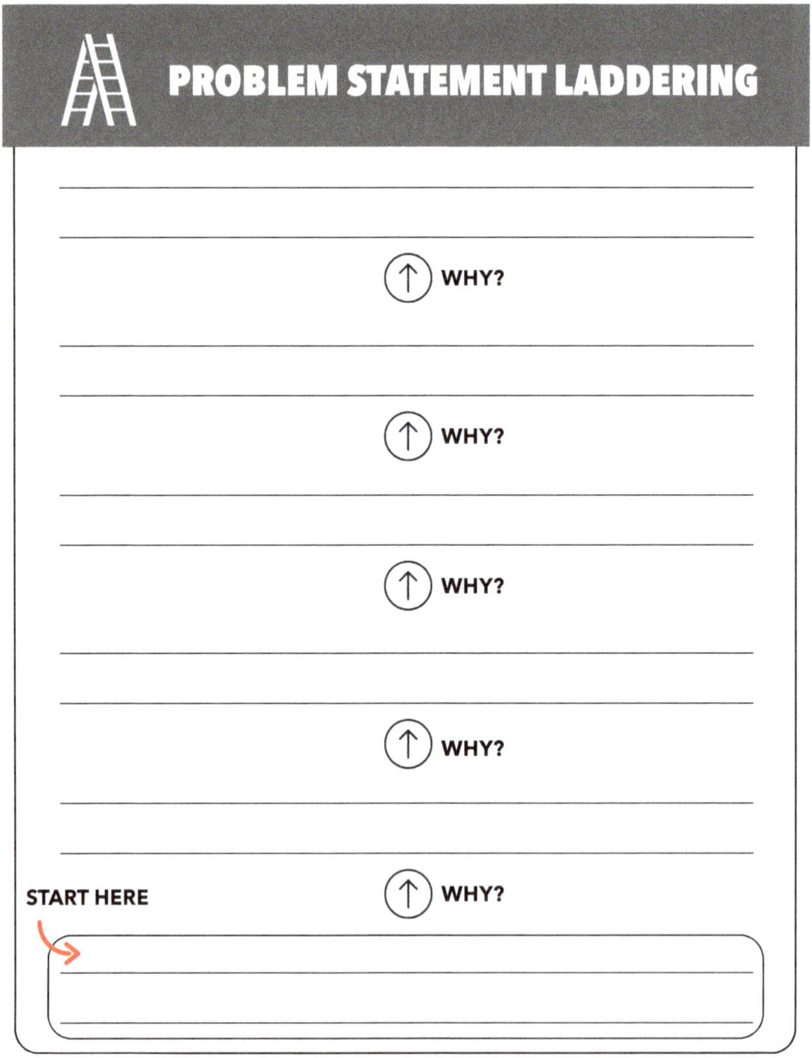

Figure 16: The 5 Whys

In the example about the two-way exchange discovery, the first question is, "**Why** did the subject change their mind on being open to life insurance?" The answer was because they recognized a need they didn't know they had. Well, **why** was that? They thought about it deeply. **Why** was that? Because they took the needed amount of time to do so. **Why** was that? Someone engaged them in a two-way exchange/conversation that was all about them. **Why** was that? Because we paid them to do so. While we may not be able to pay people to sit and engage, we can do experiments to determine what it would take to get people to pay attention longer and engage with something that would simulate the two-way exchange.

2. **Empathy and Active Listening:** Advisors or any other people on the front lines with clients and the public should continuously strive to become better listeners and more empathetic communicators. Again, this idea is straightforward, but few really master it. Empathy comes from truly putting yourself in the shoes of another person and feeling how they do, even if you have no shared experience. Additionally, active listening is a byproduct of curiosity. When you are genuinely curious, without an agenda, you can find out new things that you didn't know before.
3. **Invest in Soft Skills Training:** Invest in training programs that enhance your soft skills, such as empathy, active listening, and effective communication. Yes, these can be taught.

4. **Maintain Regular Contact with the "No Thank Yous":** Regularly check in with clients, even if they initially declined to purchase life insurance. Circumstances change, and consistent engagement can lead to future opportunities. More importantly, it shows that you care. Set reminders and put aside time just for this type of activity, or augment your team and make it someone else's job.

5. **Personalize Communication (for Real):** Tailor interactions to each client's unique needs and concerns. This level of personalization builds trust and shows clients that their advisor genuinely cares about their well-being. It's tempting to cut time and cost by engaging in blast communication, letting the technology pretend to personalize it with their name and some kind of common issue that most people want to address. However, taking the time to customize anything that is supposed to be a two-way exchange, with details that only apply to that person *(e.g., "I know your son, David, has just turned three")* will give you a much higher return on your investment of time. And of course, you need to know these personal details as well, not just rely on the technology to spit it out into an email or text. Even if you know it long enough to have a conversation about it and then forget later, that's okay. After all, we are human!

6. **Balance Human Interaction and Technology:** Leverage the strength of human empathy and emotion with the strength of technology. While technology can streamline processes and improve efficiency, human interaction remains crucial and is the only way to truly connect in a meaningful way. It's okay to use technology for the things people expect you to use it for. That's a given, but don't try to inject efficiency into the parts that it does a half-baked job with.

CHAPTER FIVE

THE UNIQUE ROLE OF EMPATHY

"Oh, why you look so sad? / Tears are in your eyes / Come on and come to me now / Don't be ashamed to cry / Let me see you through / Cause I've seen the dark side, too."

–THE PRETENDERS,
"I'll Stand by You," 1994

Empathy is a term that gets tossed around frequently, especially in today's fast-paced, digitally-connected world where everyone wants us to have more of it. I agree on that point, but let's slow down for a moment and really dissect what empathy means. Empathy is more than just feeling sorry for someone or offering polite condolences. It's *not* sympathy. It's about truly connecting with another person on an emotional level—understanding their feelings, their fears, their hopes, and their experiences. It's about seeing the world through their eyes, even when their world is vastly different from your own.

In the world of business, and especially in industries like life insurance, this kind of emotional connection is often seen as secondary to facts, figures, and sales tactics. However, here's the truth: empathy is the secret sauce. It's the glue that holds relationships together and transforms a simple transaction into a lifelong partnership. Let's take a step back in time. There was a day when life insurance sales were naturally empathetic when connection and community were the cornerstones of doing business. Imagine the door-to-door insurance salesman of the 1950s, a fixture in the neighborhood. These salesmen, known as debit agents, didn't just peddle policies—they built relationships. They knew their clients by name, they checked in on the kids, and they collected premiums face-to-face. The sale wasn't really about pressure or fear; it was about trust and connection.

They were part of the community. They were welcomed into homes and listened to the worries and concerns of their clients. This level of interaction wasn't just about business; it was social. These agents were trusted, not because they were good at closing deals, but because they were good at connecting with people. *(The well-known 1950s TV sitcom called Father Knows Best starred Robert Young and Jane Wyatt. Robert Young played the lead role of Jim Anderson, a well-respected person in the community, sage advisor to his kids, and he also happened to be an insurance agent. While not everyone could be as respected as Jim, it demonstrated the difference in the perception of such professionals.)*

As time went on, the nature of these sales began to change. Things sped up. Time spent with people gave way to efficiency, automation, and a more transactional approach so that more money could be made inside the same timeframe. Spending time getting to know people took a backseat. The result? Sales became more about the numbers and less about the people. The intimate, relationship-driven nature of the business faded, replaced by a more impersonal, distant approach where being face-to-face was more of a nuisance. As that shift occurred, so, too, did the rise of the stigma around salespeople—that they were pushy, manipulative, and driven purely by getting the sale.

Yet, now more than ever, empathy is critical. We live in a world where meaningful human connection is rare, where people are bombarded with information and yet starved for true understanding. In this environment, empathy isn't just a nice-to-have; it's a necessity. It's what sets you apart from the competition. It's what turns a cold call into a warm relationship and a product pitch into a genuine conversation about needs and values. Consumers have wised up and know when they're being pitched to.

EMPATHY AS A CORE TENET OF TRUST, NOW MORE THAN EVER

We live in a time where technology allows us to connect with people all over the world in an instant, yet those connections often lack depth. Social media, live streams, and influencers dominate our lives, creating a constant flow of surface-level interactions. However, when it comes to real human connection, the kind that builds trust and loyalty, technology alone isn't enough. How could it be? Machines cannot and should not do that.

Recent events, specifically the pandemic known as COVID-19, snapped this fact into focus rather quickly and abruptly. Think about where you were when you found out we all had to start sheltering in place. Most of us had never even heard about that protocol before. At that moment, we all started fearing things we used to see as givens...the food supply, socialization, even toilet paper! It's like we were all forcibly pushed downward on Maslow's hierarchy of needs all at the same time, worrying about the basics more than the privileges of self-actualization. As a result, we started making more decisions based on our gut instincts versus logic. Hence, trust—and empathy—played a bigger role now than ever before. As of the time of this writing in 2025, we have not yet gone back to the way it was prior to COVID, and if anything, the world is still vulnerable and susceptible to making decisions on gut emotions rather than logic.

In today's world, consumers are more discerning than ever. They're not just buying products; they're buying experiences. They're looking for brands and businesses that see them as more than just a number on a spreadsheet. They want to feel understood, valued, and heard. But, as stated before, empathy must be real. It can't be manufactured. It must come from a genuine place of wanting to connect with others on a human level. I once spoke at a prominent industry event, revealing an entire study about empathy and how consumers want that from their advisors. One gentleman asked, "How can I make the client believe that I'm empathetic?" That question alone showed how disconnected he was from the true meaning of empathy. If you're trying to make someone believe you're empathetic, you've already missed the point. Empathy isn't a strategy or a tactic—it's a way of being. It's about showing up as your authentic self and connecting with others in a way that is honest, sincere, and caring.

The days of fear-based sales tactics are over. Remember the old “backing up the hearse” technique we discussed in Chapter Three, where advertisements showed crying widows and fatherless children to scare people into buying life insurance? Those tactics might have worked in the past, but today’s consumers are much savvier. They’re tired of being manipulated, and they can see through inauthentic sales pitches designed to play on people’s emotions in a way that leaves them feeling terrible. What they’re looking for now is someone who understands their concerns, really listens, and helps them make decisions that are in their best interest.

What I found fascinating about Dunbar’s theory, which was mentioned in the previous chapter, is that it highlights the limits of the human brain when it comes to maintaining meaningful connections. It shows that we can only handle so many relationships before becoming overwhelmed or coming across as inauthentic. For example, if I forget your name after meeting you six months ago, it’s a sign that we don’t have a strong connection. Sure, we could start over, but it might mean replacing someone else in that limited circle of 150 people to make room for you. It’s not an exact science, but you get the idea—you almost have to let go of one relationship to maintain another.

Things that aren’t rooted in logic—like empathy and emotions—aren’t typically taught. The brain has different parts for different functions: the logical part, the emotional part, and the instinctual part. But often, we’re governed by the latter part that is focused on survival, which is often rooted in the very dominant emotion of fear. But there’s an even more powerful emotion that we must understand and treat with care. Shame.

NUANCE 12: The Relationship between Shame, Judgment, and Empathy

Shame is one of the most powerful and destructive human emotions to exist. I learned this nuance from Brené Brown, thought leader, researcher, speaker, and author. If you have not heard of her, please Google her and watch a few of her Ted Talks or listen to some of her podcasts. She's the poster child for authenticity, making the word "shit show" a household term, but she's also brilliant in how she can communicate the human condition and help us navigate it.

Shame is that deep, gnawing feeling that tells you that you're not good enough, that you're flawed or broken in some fundamental way. There are many facets of shame that I learned about in Brené's book called *Atlas of the Heart*. Unfortunately, shame often finds its way into the sales process, especially in industries like life insurance, where people are dealing with deeply personal and often uncomfortable topics like death, illness, and financial security. It can be triggered by what is perceived as judgment. In fact, according to a Maddock Douglas study done in 2018, the concern of being judged by a financial professional was true for over 75% of subjects.

Most people can tell when you're judging them or others. It's like getting a weird dopamine rush from something negative. It gives you this false sense of superiority, making you feel like you're smarter than others or that you're better *(or not as bad)*. These feelings of superiority feed into the ego, but real life isn't like that.

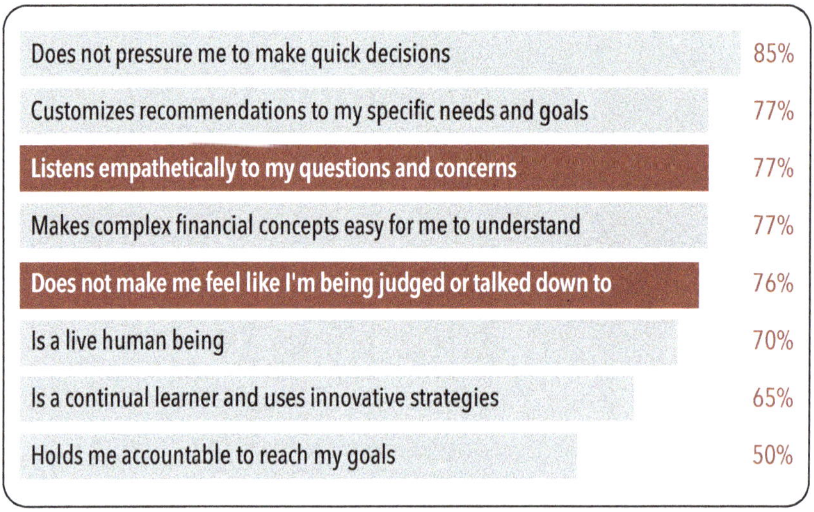

Figure 17: Maddock Douglas and AALU, The Future of the Life Insurance Industry, 2018 "Imagine the ideal source of advice for you personally. How important are these attributes?"

There's actually a German word for this feeling—*Schadenfreude*. It's the strange happiness you get from seeing something embarrassing happen to someone else. You might think, "Wow, that's awful for them," but part of you feels slightly satisfied about it. For example, these situations might include when a celebrity looks bad in a photo, an Olympic skater falls on their butt, or someone embarrasses themselves in a *Funniest Home Videos* segment. People love to watch those "fail" situations where no one gets seriously hurt, but they look foolish. We all laugh because it's funny, but that's *Schadenfreude* at play.

Wisdom tells us it's not our place to pass judgment on others, which is especially important when trying to build empathy with customers. Judging someone for their choices, like a person living paycheck to paycheck who chooses to buy a flat-screen TV instead of term insurance, doesn't help us. *(I can't tell you how many times, even up till the time of this writing, that I have heard insurance company executives judging their potential customers for their choices of what they spend their money on.)* There could be many reasons for their decision, and empathy requires us to understand them without judgment.

Right now, there's a huge societal gap in empathy—really, it's become a chasm. Shame plays a big role here. Unlike guilt, which is about feeling bad for something you did, shame makes you feel like you're a terrible person at your core. That distinction is critical because shame can deepen that empathy gap even further.

One important note to consider, however, is that empathy can transform shame. Where shame isolates and tears people down, empathy connects and builds people up. When we approach our clients with empathy, we're not just selling them a product; we're offering them understanding, support, and validation. We're saying, "I see you. I hear you. I understand your fears and concerns." That simple act of empathy can make all the difference in the world.

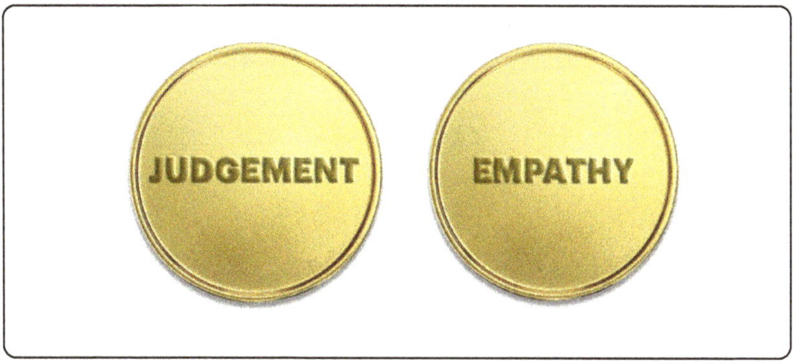

Figure 18: Empathy can transform Judgement like two sides of the same coin.

It's like two sides of a coin. On one side, you have judgment and shame. On the other side, you have empathy and connection. As professionals in the life insurance industry, it's our job to help our clients flip that coin. It's our job to help them move from a place of fear and shame—where the conversations are often heavy and the decisions are deeply personal and can get really dark—to a place of understanding and empowerment.

EMPATHY CAN BE TAUGHT

One of the most common questions I get asked is, "Can empathy be taught?" The answer is a resounding yes. Empathy isn't some mystical, elusive quality that only a select few possess. It's a skill that can be developed and strengthened over time. In an industry like life insurance, where emotions run high and the stakes are personal, empathy is a skill that everyone needs to cultivate, and that can take time. I am not suggesting that it's easy or that everyone can learn it. But if you or someone you know is interested in building this skill, then there's a great chance that they are teachable.

So, how do we teach empathy? It starts with the basics—listening, *really* listening. Not just hearing the words that someone is saying but understanding the meaning behind them. It's about making eye contact, giving feedback, and hearing and understanding people, without your own agenda or waiting for what you are going to say next. It's about putting yourself in the other person's shoes, even if you've never walked that path yourself. Does that mean you can't convey empathy over the phone or text? No, but it does mean those physical barriers can make it harder to show people that you care. If someone called you on your birthday to simply say, "Happy birthday," and then hung up, you wouldn't think that person cared very much at all about you. However, if someone called you to talk about you, ask how you were doing, and they remembered that event you were presenting at and asked you how you did, then that shows that they care enough to remember your previous conversation.

Empathy also means understanding the risks and fears that come with making decisions. In the world of life insurance, clients are often dealing with fear—fear of the unknown, fear of making the wrong decision, fear of facing their own mortality, or even fear of being judged for what they did or didn't purchase. As advisors, it's our job to guide them through that fear with empathy and understanding, to help them make decisions that are in their best interest, not just ours.

Herein lies the challenge: the very nature of sales, especially in a commission-driven industry like life insurance, can make empathy difficult. When you're focused on meeting your quotas and hitting your targets, it's easy to let your lizard brain take over—the part of your brain that's all about survival, fight or flight. When that shift happens, empathy can go out the window, instead replaced by an aggressive, pushy, or needy sales approach. The destructive emotions at play in the agents' heads are in the way of them helping their clients with their own destructive emotions. *(Wow, that's heavy, man!)*

It doesn't have to be that way, however. Empathy can be trained. Possessing this skill frankly sets one advisor apart from another in a very profound way.

WALKING IN THE SHOES OF THE CUSTOMER

One of the most powerful ways to develop empathy is by walking in the shoes of your customers—literally and figuratively. When you take the time to truly understand what your clients are going through, you gain a deeper appreciation for their fears, concerns, and needs. You see the world through their eyes, and that ability allows you to connect with them on a much deeper level than you would by just trying to sell them a product or service.

My colleagues and I once worked with a health insurance company that was committed to becoming more client-centric. They didn't just talk about empathy—they put it into action. Together, we created a massive empathy training program that involved every single employee, from those on the front lines to those in the executive suites. We built an entire experience "room" where employees could walk a mile in their customers' shoes—literally. They went through a maze where they experienced what it was like to have a vision problem and not be able to read the fine print on a bill, or to have a hearing problem and struggle with an automated phone system. It was an eye-opening experience for everyone involved, and it made a real difference in how they interacted with their customers. The program went way beyond this particular example and included many new behavioral shifts that at first glance seemed like "fluff," but it translated to the bottom line in a profound way.

There's a great story about how empathy transformed a near disaster in the book, *Plan D*, by my business partner and friend, Mike Maddock. His friend, Christina, took a job to pay for college tuition at a collection agency. The upshot of the culture there was that people were super nice in the lunchroom and super mean on the phone. They used all kinds of shame tactics to try and get people to pay their debts. Then, one day, a man came to the door, visibly agitated, having gotten one too many of these threatening calls. She had the honor of answering that door. He said he had a gun and was going to shoot someone there. Somehow, Christina had the wherewithal to show him empathy instead of screaming and lashing out. As a result, he paid his debt and left. After that, she realized that maybe there was a better way to do this job.

So, she opened her own collection agency utilizing empathy as a core component of the experience. She spent way more time than her competitors did on empathy training, measured success by how many people thanked the team, and did many other untraditional things that were all steeped in empathy and compassion. She crushed her competition, collecting more debts owed than the other collection agencies. That shows you that there is a better way to get the desired results, and that we cannot just "write off" irresponsible financial behavior as unchangeable. It's not easy, but empathy makes almost anything possible.

Empathy isn't a one-time event, though. It's not something you can check off a list and be done with it. It's an ongoing commitment, something that needs to be nurtured and reinforced over time. That means continuously training and retraining your employees by putting them in situations where they can develop and practice empathy.

I experienced fake empathy recently, and it left me cold.

NUANCE 13: It's Weird to Try and Automate Empathy

One day, I had to make a call to a bank about a mortgage I had paid off and was feeling a little frustrated about it. I was owed a final escrow check and hadn't received it yet. The first thing the representative said to me was, "Congratulations on paying off your mortgage." That didn't feel right to me, even if I hadn't been frustrated. "Congratulations" might make sense if I was still living in the same home that mortgage was on, but that's not what happened. I only paid off my mortgage because I sold my house. You are supposed to pay off your mortgage when you don't own a home anymore. It's kinda the rule, right? And what if it had been under negative circumstances, such as after a divorce, a death, or a bankruptcy? It just felt so "off" and obviously wasn't genuine. It would have been better not to try and show any empathy at all than to manufacture it with a set of automated prompts that led them to a false conclusion.

AI likely flagged it as an achievement that should make me feel proud, but that wasn't how I felt. I wasn't upset about it, but the comment just didn't resonate with me at all. Then, the longer it took for me to get my escrow check, the more I *was* feeling upset.

These kinds of missteps happen all the time. Humans can make them, too, if they're not engaging in a genuine, two-way exchange. Once someone really understands the situation, they can respond authentically, but it has to come from a real place.

Let's dive deeper into listening skills. A good technique I've found is by demonstrating the antithesis, which we can probably all agree on. *(I think, anyway!)* Presidential debates. These televised events have become the deliberate opposite of active listening. Questions are asked, and answers are immediately spun into promoting another agenda. Why? Because there's a fear that an authentic answer might make someone look bad politically. Back in my days as a spokesperson for insurance companies who was interviewed on news programs, I had media training. They trained me *not* to answer direct questions but to have a series of talking points ready to dive into. For instance, the interviewer would ask a question, and then I would say, "That's a great question, and what's even more important is ____________________." Then, I would get to say whatever I wanted without actually answering the question at all.

Is there any question why there's such a lack of trust of political figures? It's important to remember that when we witness these debates and interviews, we are not really witnessing a two-way exchange unless both parties are agreeing on *actually* listening to each other and answering questions with both respect and empathy. When you watch a great interview with a political figure *(often after they leave office)*, you get a feeling of, "Wow, I have more respect for that person than I did when he/she was in office." The reason? They are authentically and empathetically engaging in the conversation as opposed to pushing their own agenda.

A TOOL FOR TEACHING EMPATHY

In an effort to help professionals strengthen their empathy, my colleagues created what we affectionately call the "Empathy Mad Lib." For those of you not familiar with a Mad Lib, it's a word game that has paragraphs containing blank spaces, and you're supposed to fill them in to create your own unique story.

EMPATHY MAD-LIB

PROFILE

PERSONAL NAME	AGE
FAMILY STATUS	OCCUPATION
OTHER DETAILS	

STORY

1 On a typical day, I wake up around ______________ (TIME).

2 The first thing I do is ______________ (ACTIVITY) and then i go to ______________ (LOCATION).

3 The best part of my day is ______________ (ACTIVITY) because ______________ (REASON).

4 I wish I could spend less time on ______________ (ACTIVITY) and more time on ______________ (ACTIVITY).

5 If I had a magic want to change one thing in the world, I would ______________ (VERB).

Figure 19: The Empathy Mad Lib

When we think about empathy, that story is always about someone else. Oftentimes, when we are caught up in our own heads, the needs of other people become elusive. You may become annoyed with someone driving too slowly in front of you or stopping without warning. How do you know it's not because they are having an asthma attack or other medical emergency? You really don't and may never know for sure. If you can imagine a reason for what you might have been potentially judging them about, the judgment falls away to a more positive experience for both parties.

The Empathy Mad Lib is designed to do just that. It's a story about someone else, and you can pick the persona. You need to pick someone who you or your team might "judge" or stereotype in some way, however. One example might be a scruffy twenty-nine-year-old man by the name of Dave. He carries a backpack, bikes around town, and wears loose clothing that looks worn out. Some people may think he's not even worth trying to pursue. He appears as though he doesn't have any money, or maybe as if he doesn't even have anyone he cares about.

But what if that were not true at all? Could you make up a different story about Dave? Imagine he wakes up at 7 a.m. every day, then goes to his computer to check on how his new platform fared overnight. He started a tech company when he was twenty-two because he's been trying to raise money for education in underprivileged areas of the world. The best part of his day is when he takes his afternoon bike ride to clear his head and think. He wishes he could spend less time having to re-convince his investors about the merits of his platform and more time on what he can be doing to advance his cause. If he had a magic wand, he'd want everyone in the world to have access to great education and a better life.

This Dave is very different from the Dave we might have judged on the surface. Even though this story is completely made up, we suddenly have more empathy for him and maybe even want to help him achieve his goals.

I've used this simple exercise with groups of people in our industry in the past, and I am surprised every time by how emotional people can get after they do it. It changes people's perspectives, for sure.

THE BIG TO-DO

Putting Money Where Our Mouth Is: Corporate Commitment to Empathy

If we're serious about developing empathy in our industry, it has to be more than just a buzzword. It has to be woven into the fabric of our organizations. That means putting money where our mouth is by investing in empathy training, creating a culture that values connection, and committing to incorporating empathy in everything we do.

However, one important thing to remember is that empathy isn't just about making the customer experience better—it's about making the work experience better, too. When employees feel valued and understood, when they know that their company is committed to creating an empathic environment where they can feel safe and valued, it creates a positive ripple effect throughout the organization. It improves employee morale, strengthens client relationships, and ultimately leads to better business outcomes.

So, what does that look like in practice?

1. It means building **empathy training** into your onboarding process and making it a core part of your company culture. It means creating opportunities for employees to walk in the shoes of your clients and truly understand their experiences. It means fostering a culture of listening, where employees feel heard and valued and empathy is celebrated as a key skill.

2. It also means **holding yourself accountable**. If you're going to commit to empathy, you have to live that commitment every day. You have to be willing to invest in your people, to prioritize their well-being, and to create a work environment where empathy is the norm, not the exception. Call people out when they are not being empathetic, too—and let them call you out, too!

At the end of the day, empathy is more than just a feel-good concept. It's a human skill that can transform your business. Remember that empathy is a skill that can always be improved. You can never be too good at listening, too good at understanding, or too good at connecting with others. *(Being too good at listening, understanding, and connecting is the new being too rich, LOL!)*

CHAPTER SIX

AI VS. HUMAN AND THE RIGHT DIVISION OF LABOR

"It wears me out / And if I could be who you wanted / If I could be who you wanted / All the time."

–RADIOHEAD,
"Fake Plastic Trees," 1995

Here's another connection between music I love and a topic I am passionate about. But if the shoe *(almost)* fits, I say you can wear it *(for a while, until it really hurts)*.

That said, this song is about how hard it is to live up to the perceived expectations of others. Radiohead is also very in tune with dystopian outcomes from technological and societal advances. The reason I think this particular song is relevant is that we are always striving for perfection, and we turn to technology to make us better. But sometimes, we can go too far. Not just with what we use it for, but for what we expect it to do.

For a long time, the industry has talked about whether or not technology will take the job of a human. At this point, I hope that we all agree the answer is no. Not even if AI was able to do a perfect job. Because it's still just a Computer, OK?

Currently, the industry sits in a transitional state, where trying to find the right balance between maintaining a hands-on approach while also taking advantage of all that technology has to offer is both imperative and incredibly difficult. Questions formed by fear swarm around our minds as we try to navigate this new frontier, but I'd like to point out that certain elements will never change. We can use these elements to help us define the future of life insurance more effectively.

This chapter delves into how we can harness the strengths of both humanity and technology to achieve the best possible outcomes. By understanding the inherent strengths and weaknesses of AI and humans, we can strategically assign tasks to the party that is best suited to complete them, ensuring that neither is misused and that both are maximized for their true potential.

THE ROLE OF TECHNOLOGY IN UNDERSTANDING CONSUMER INTENT

Technology has revolutionized the way large corporations and industries track consumer behavior. AI can analyze vast amounts of data, keep records of online searches, and even predict when a consumer might be ready to purchase a product like life insurance. For instance, if someone repeatedly searches for options for life insurance, it is a strong indicator that they are interested and likely ready to engage with a human agent or buy online *(likely having had a two-way exchange somewhere before)*. However, while AI can identify these patterns, it cannot replace the nuanced understanding that a human brings to a conversation, especially when it comes to products that involve deeply personal and financial considerations.

The tax benefits of life insurance, particularly permanent life insurance, are a prime example of where human expertise is irreplaceable. While AI can calculate and present these benefits to potential consumers, only a human can truly explain the implications to a family, understand the clients' unique financial situations, and provide tailored advice based on the consumers' circumstances.

NUANCE 14: Irrational vs. Rational

The decision to purchase life insurance is driven by more than just numbers—it involves the emotional responsibility of caring for loved ones, a factor AI cannot adequately address.

The Spectrum of Rational and Irrational Decision-Making

In the realm of decision-making, there exists a spectrum ranging from the completely rational to the entirely irrational. When we say "irrational," we don't mean it's bad or invalid. Rather, it means it's based more on emotions than facts. On the rational end *(the right side)*, we find tasks that are rooted in facts and logic. Being accurate and efficient, possibly even probabilistic, these are areas where AI excels. However, as we move towards the irrational end of the spectrum *(the left side)*, empathy, authenticity, and individual circumstances become the crux of the job, and the role of human agents therefore becomes indispensable.

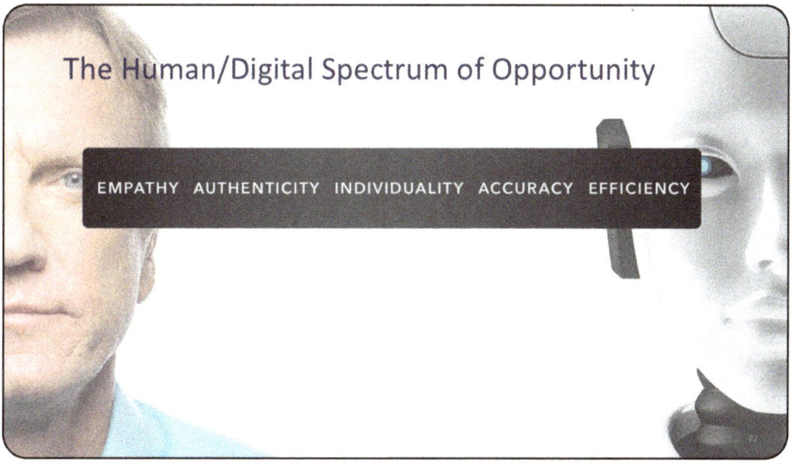

Figure 20: From Irrational To Rational; The Human/Digital Spectrum of Opportunity

AI can assist in understanding individuality to a certain extent. It can gather data on a person's demographics, lifestyle, family structure, and financial status. However, it cannot grasp all the nuances that make someone feel like their uniqueness is understood. Without that need being met, empathy can't be felt. For this reason, the middle of the spectrum must be carefully shared by AI and humanity.

NUANCE 15: Authenticity, Getting Real Already

The word "authenticity" is frequently used these days and has become part of the lexicon of the business world. People use it to tell others what they are doing right and also use it as a criticism for what they are doing wrong. It's sometimes used as a synonym for letting one's freak flag fly, and it can even be the justification for acting like a jerk sometimes. But the true meaning of authenticity is being real, true to oneself, and visibly real by others. Even if you are being a jerk, when it's rooted in what's true for you, it's somehow more acceptable.

In business, however, authenticity is a little more of a delicate balance. I've often described it as an intersection between your passion, your professionalism, and your personality.

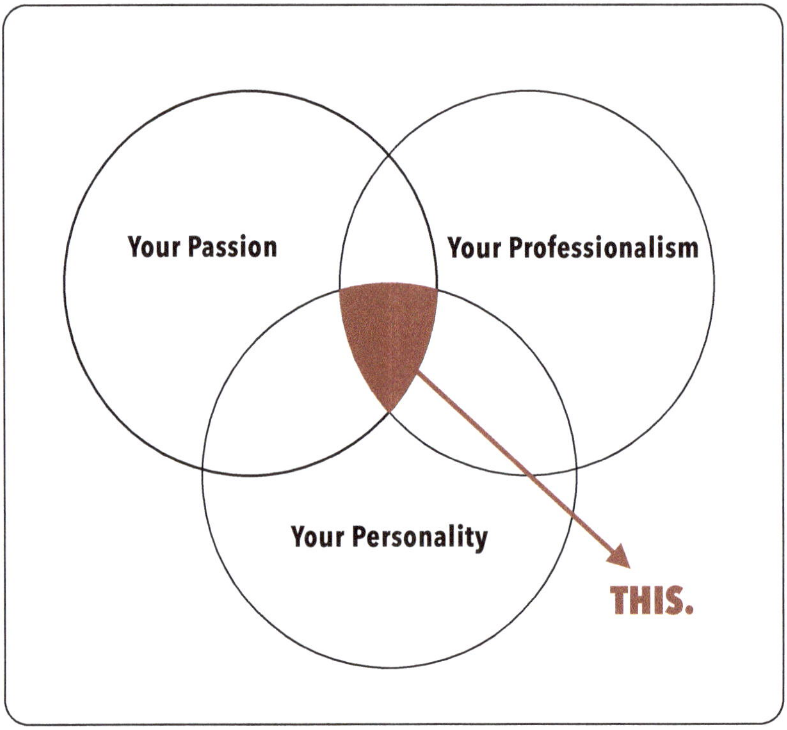

One of the key challenges facing the life insurance industry is the lack of authentic communication. When people are trained to memorize scripts or are given tips about language that "works," it might be helpful. On the other hand, it also might be a recipe for being a second-rate version of someone else instead of a first-rate version of yourself.

Studies have shown that consumers often find the language used by insurers confusing and impersonal. When people spew industry-specific jargon and ignore that the other person is not comfortable with the conversation, that's not cool. Authentic communication, however, is more than just simplifying or "dumbing down" the language being used; it involves several elements, in fact. In a widely used study done by Maddock Douglas and LIMRA in 2014, there are actually six elements to authentic communication, which are:

1. **Easy to Understand:** Use everyday language that resonates with consumers.
2. **Down to Earth:** Incorporate realistic images and scenarios that consumers can relate to.
3. **Memorable:** Craft communication that is interesting and engaging and that sticks.
4. **Positive:** Deliver messages that are warm and comforting.
5. **Credible:** Ensure that the sources of information are trustworthy and coming from a place of the consumers' best interests.
6. **Relevant:** Show that the company understands the consumers' unique needs and circumstances.

Here's a bit more detail on each element.

EASY TO UNDERSTAND

One research subject said this quote when presented with the typical pile of information involved in selling life insurance: "I was overwhelmed...my brain shut down."

Easy to understand relates to simple, everyday language. Consumers prefer layman's terms over industry jargon. People like to do their own legwork when they begin the research or shopping process, so it is essential to make the information easy to understand. For many, the first step is to Google it. Even those who work with advisors commonly do their own research online.

Think of it as a confidence builder. When they understand the information being presented, their confidence rises, and their comfort level grows. Even if a person believes that he needs life insurance, he may not feel comfortable enough to take that next step if he doesn't fully understand how it works. If people understand it, they are more likely to move forward. How do we change our approach to help people understand the fundamentals without overwhelming them with information they don't really need to make a wise choice?

One subject summed it up well by saying. "Make this understandable to people who don't do this for a living."

DOWN TO EARTH

Another subject said the following when presented with "ideal" images of retirement: "In order to plan for your own retirement, you have to be in a certain economic class...they promise we can have this lifestyle once we retire, and I don't think that's realistic."

How do we create imagery that conveys realistic goals rather than those based on some manufactured ideal? Being down-to-earth is about being real, human, and approachable. This element is also a very visual one. Communication can be more than just words on a page; it can also include images. Images do not necessarily need to mirror the consumer's current perceptions, but they must seem realistic and attainable. As an example, people most closely associate retirement investments with words that conjure a sense of security, like "savings" and "nest egg." Words like "vacations" and "relaxing" are not often thought of.

One reason behind this association is that people are worried about having enough for a secure retirement and being comfortable. Many feel that relaxation and vacations during this stage of their lives are unattainable. Yet, what images do company retirement websites often use? People relaxing and taking vacations, seemingly without a care in the world. *(Frankly, if I see one more Adirondack chair in a retirement ad, I might scream!)*

MEMORABLE

When reading a brochure about life insurance, another subject said, "When you started reading deep into it, it got a little like, 'What are they talking about?'...When you got into stuff, it just kind of bored you."

To be memorable means to be interesting and refreshing. In talking to consumers, we found that the more tedious and confusing they find the source to be, the less likely they are to continue and retain what they read. This fact holds true for statements, newsletters, and websites. Consider the customer experience with other types of products and services. How do customers stay engaged? How does this kind of memorable engagement compare to life insurance companies? Insurers likely have less interaction with their customers than other companies would have. For many, the only communication is billing notices and policy changes.

How do we cut through the clutter of daily life and engage with consumers in a way that sticks?

Here's where we could take a lesson from other industries. My favorite? Diamonds. How much should you spend on a diamond engagement ring? Most people know it's some multiple of your salary. Two times? Three times? But the bigger question is, "How do they know that?" If you ask, most people are not sure how they do. They just do. Ad executives would say it is the brilliance of the ad campaign from DeBeers, which launched decades ago. Yes, that's true, but there's a nuance here, too. What they did was take the familiar (a paycheck) and use it to describe the unfamiliar (buying the right diamond). This connection is what made it stick!

POSITIVE

Another subject of the study said the following quote about the overall message of life insurance: "Offer a little bit of sunshine with it—it doesn't have to be a scary thing."

Being positive is an expression of warmth, comfort, and encouragement. By being positive, you can combine reality with possibility. The first thing that comes to mind when people think of life insurance is death. We need to reframe that mindset, refocus it, and find the good in it for consumers. This tactic can include the acknowledgment of their good health, their ability to qualify for high amounts of protection, and even the value that comes with keeping a permanent policy. Similar opportunities exist with retirement planning. While the image of owning a sailboat may look unrealistic to the average consumer today, remind them that the sooner they prepare for retirement, the more realistic that future becomes. In many aspects of life, language has a profound effect on the ability to keep people engaged and to build rapport. Positivity keeps the conservation going. How do we find positives about life insurance? Another participant described it this way: "We're talking about something ending; we already know how bad that is. Maybe not use such heavy words with it."

CREDIBLE

When thinking about actually making the purchase, another participant said this: "I need to talk to someone who knows insurance inside and out." Furthermore, another person said the following: "Too much verbiage. Makes me think they're trying to hide something from the public."

The element of credibility has two primary aspects: expertise and trust. Expertise determines if the consumers believe that the company—or the advisor—has the correct knowledge to offer the proper advice. Trust decides if the consumers feel the company—or advisor—has their best interests at heart. Many consumers are not convinced that companies and advisors are in it to help them. In fact, only a small percentage of people feel that life insurers have their best interests in mind. Consequently, there is a pretty low level of credibility and trust among consumers, which negatively impacts the industry. Trust is a major factor when consumers choose an advisor or company with which to do business, and without it, a successful relationship is nearly, if not totally, impossible.

How else can we show the general public that we are putting the consumer first?

RELEVANT

When working through a pile of form letters and collateral, one participant said: "It didn't seem like it was identifying me personally…I didn't think they were talking to me. Did they do that on purpose?"

Relevance is about people feeling that the company knows, understands, and is specifically talking to them. This element of authenticity is a major motivating factor for people during the shopping process. Many consumers think companies are communicating to someone else instead of to them; as a result, these organizations fail to connect with consumers, especially with Generation Y. Remember, competitors today are not just other financial service companies; they are also retailers. Consumers expect the same level of customer experience with insurance companies as they get with other companies. Insurers need to understand their target markets and communicate with them in a way that makes it feel like a personalized experience. Another key point to keep in mind is that relevancy changes based on which generation the consumer belongs to. Boomers think companies are talking to a younger audience, and Generation Y (aka millennials) feels that the intended targets are older people. Generation X is more likely to believe companies are targeting them. Recognize that one size does not fit all.

How do we create dialogue that considers who consumers are as individuals?

AUTHENTICITY IN PRACTICE

Not clear what it is/Jargony	LOW	1	2	3	4	5	HIGH	**EASY TO UNDERSTAND** Clear what it is/ Everyday Words
Unachievable/ Unrealistic success picture	LOW	1	2	3	4	5	HIGH	**DOWN TO EARTH** Achievable/Realistic success picture
Forgettable	LOW	1	2	3	4	5	HIGH	**MEMORABLE** Differentiated / "Sticky"
Leaves you feeling bad	LOW	1	2	3	4	5	HIGH	**POSITIVE** Leaves recipient with good/em-powered feeling
Only for the benefit of the communicator	LOW	1	2	3	4	5	HIGH	**CREDIBLE** In their best interests
Sent/said to anyone	LOW	1	2	3	4	5	HIGH	**RELEVANT** Meant specifically for the recipient

Figure 21: The Authenticity Scoring Tool

As you think about key communications, such as email templates, letters, bills, etc., that act as important touchpoints for consumers, take a critical look at how they fare on each of those six elements. My colleagues created the authenticity scoring tool for this purpose, enabling you to see the distinctions between what's great (5), bad (1), and just "meh" (3). At the time of the study, the industry scored "meh" for both life insurance and retirement communications. However, since then, authenticity has improved greatly, likely driven by the industry's desire to be more current. Insurtech startups have really helped raise the bar in that regard. Bravo!

A PERSONAL STORY ABOUT THE POWER OF AUTHENTICITY

Quite by accident, in an attempt to be funny in a keynote speech, I poked fun at our industry by showing this fake book cover for my first book. The title is *How to Sell Life Insurance to People on Airplanes*. I said that if you need peace and quiet on your plane ride home to read, just wrap this cover around any book, and nobody would bother you!

Figure 22: The travel accessory for the peace and quiet one needs to read on a plane

It wasn't real...until it was. People started asking me for it. So, one day on a long car ride, my husband, Jim, and I started writing the liner notes for this book cover. It took all of fifteen minutes. Then, we had our creative team make it real. The next thing I knew, people were grabbing them in droves. One of our clients, Scott Campbell *(who is hilariously funny)*, took it with him on a plane and took a selfie. He posted the picture on social media, and it started a trend.

That meant I had to do it, too, right? I couldn't let others take the risk while I wasn't walking the walk. So, when Jim and I were taking our next flight, I said, "We have to wrap our books now and get a selfie on that plane." No sooner did we wrap a book with that cover than a random guy came up to us, laughing, and asked if we would take a picture with him and the book cover. I asked, "Why are you so interested in this?"

He responded, "Well, I am with Northwestern Mutual, and I think it's hilarious."

I said, "Oh, wow, now *that* makes sense," and we posed for a pic with him.

But seconds later, something amazing happened. Another guy came up to us and said, "Hey, can I get a picture, too?"

I asked, "Are you also with Northwestern Mutual?"

He said, "No, I just think it's funny."

After we took the photo, the Northwestern Mutual guy said, "Do you have life insurance?"

The other guy said, "No, but I probably should..."

Then, before we knew it, cards were exchanged, the flip happened, and Jim and I looked at each other and said, "OMG, you can't make this stuff up!"

Soon after, I started using this story in all my keynote speeches and giving these covers away as a joke. People were taking them and doing the same thing...instinctively! And you know what happened? They started emailing me that they were *actually selling life insurance on airplanes!* The people they were sitting next to laughed and then trusted the person holding the book because it addressed an unspoken element about how people really feel. There were uninterrupted, two-way exchanges loaded with individuality, authenticity, and empathy. Holy crap.

Now, it's in three languages, and there are multiple variations on the theme.

What do we take away from this story? As long as we lean in to what other people are feeling, we can let go of the irrational, assume positive intent, lower down our walls, and build trust. In this profession, accomplishing that type of connection is *mastery!*

As we consider all of the items on the spectrum of irrational to rational, it will help us better frame which jobs are best suited for the human and which are better suited to technology.

GETTING THE DIVISION OF LABOR RIGHT: HUMANS AND AI AS PARTNERS

The key to success lies in getting the division of labor between humans and AI right. It is not a question of one being better than the other; rather, it is about leveraging the strengths of both. AI should handle tasks that are data-driven, repetitive, and require high efficiency. These include tasks like capturing data accurately in an application and in a way that doesn't require multiple entries, designing algorithms that can make routine decisions based on the same fact pattern, ensuring that data is shared and cataloged appropriately, looking for patterns in the data–such as those that detect fraud–and signaling and creating follow ups and triggers for routine communications.

However, humans must handle tasks that involve empathy, creativity, and complex decision-making. These are areas where AI falls short and where human intuition and emotional intelligence shine. The human touch is essential in demand creation, as stated earlier–getting people interested in a "sold, not bought" product or service in the first place. It is nearly impossible to create genuine demand through AI alone. The reason why is because it often involves understanding and addressing the irrational fears and desires of consumers, and getting them to take action on something they likely need but don't have motivation to buy.

This collaboration can lead to a new cost model, where efficiency is maximized without sacrificing the quality of human interaction.

WHERE THE INDUSTRY IS FALLING SHORT

Despite the potential for a harmonious relationship between humans and AI, knowing the role of each is critical to success. Digital platforms have been launched with the promise of replacing human agents, but they often fall short because they cannot overcome the "invisible wall" that prevents consumers from making a purchase decision without human intervention. There's no two-way exchange, and there's a fight over the small number of people who have already flipped over the wall. The role of the agent is critical to creating the demand.

Beyond that, what about the really good, empathetic, authentic humans who are out there creating demand and trying to leverage the digital platforms, and the platform fails to deliver on the thing it's expected to do?

Consider a scenario where an insurance agent approaches a potential customer, but the timing isn't right. The customer says no, not because they don't need life insurance, but because they simply aren't ready to commit. Two months later, the customer might be ready, but if the agent fails to follow up, that opportunity slips away for the moment—human fail. Perhaps the agent eventually reconnects with the prospective client another two months later, and by that time, the customer is ready to buy. However, life happens—maybe something else comes up, like a family emergency or even a bout with COVID-19—and the appointment gets pushed back again. Then, finally, the customer is contacted one more time, and the buying process begins. They start going through the application process online, and it becomes so cumbersome and redundant—tech fail—that the client gives up once again, delays, or drags their feet. Then, a health issue happens. The client becomes uninsurable. Too late. Game over—everyone fails.

TECH'S PRIMARY ROLE: ACT QUICKLY, DON'T SCREW UP

"She's come undone / She didn't know what she was headed for / And when I found what she was headed for / It was too late."

–THE GUESS WHO,
"Undun," 1969

One of the most significant risks of relying too heavily on technology is that it can undo the hard work of human agents who created the demand in the first place. If the data used is inaccurate or outdated, it can lead to errors that frustrate consumers. The agent does all the irrational, hard work of creating demand and getting the client to act. Then, the agent provides the link to an electronic application–or executes it for the client. If a consumer has to provide the same information repeatedly because the system didn't capture it correctly the first time, it creates a negative experience. If the app doesn't have access to the same information that the client previously gave or another requirement is triggered later and the data isn't pulled from the original source, it's a huge irritation. This irritation not only diminishes trust in the tech, but also in the human agents associated with it. If simple details can't be remembered accurately, how can clients trust that the agents, and the companies they represent, will care about getting anything else right?

NUANCE 16: Where Is Tech Messing It Up?

The human's job is to create demand and build relationships. Technology should support these efforts by handling the back-end processes efficiently and without error. If tech starts to take over tasks that require empathy or decision-making, it risks creating a disconnect between the consumer and the service, leading to dissatisfaction and distrust. If the human has to get involved in the back-end portions of the process because the tech is not working properly, it's inefficient and most likely seen by the client as such. We end up losing trust points!

LOOKING FOR SAVINGS IN ALL THE WRONG PLACES

Consider this situation. An ambitious startup that aimed to revolutionize the life insurance industry promises to offer life insurance entirely online—there's no agents, no face-to-face interaction. The idea was that consumers could apply for and purchase life insurance entirely through a sleek, automated digital platform. It was a bold attempt to meet the needs of the modern, tech-savvy consumer who supposedly preferred the convenience of doing everything online.

On paper, it sounded perfect. The company invested heavily in developing a beautiful, user-friendly interface that made it easy to input information, get a quote, answer a few questions, and secure coverage quickly. The engine behind the platform was elegant and efficient, streamlining the process that typically took weeks into mere minutes.

But as promising as it seemed, the reality was quite different. Despite all the investment and effort put into the project, said company—and several other similar ventures—struggled to gain traction.

The problem wasn't the technology itself; it basically worked as intended. The issue was about demand creation. These startups assumed that by offering a hassle-free digital experience, consumers would flock to purchase life insurance because of how "easy" it now seemed to obtain. However, they underestimated one crucial element: the emotional push that consumers need to make a purchase in a category like life insurance. In essence, the failure was based on an unfair comparison of a negative demand category to a demand category. Google, Amazon, Zappos. Those are apples. Life insurance? It might not even be a fruit, but this topic will be covered in more detail in the next chapter.

The lesson is clear: you can't build an entire system on technology alone in an industry that fundamentally relies on trust, empathy, and personal connections to make people take action. The role of the human agent, it turns out, is indispensable for creating the demand that these digital platforms hoped would naturally arise. Some startups have since realized this concept and are now combining their digital engines with traditional human distribution networks, finding that the blend of technology and personal touch is where the real potential lies. So, the effort is not lost. However, again, we must go back to the nuance of insight and ask why, why, why, why, why! *(refer to the Five Whys in Chapter Four)*. In addition, another important thing to remember is that the "pain" of the process is real, but mostly for the agent. They deal with it day in and day out. Consumers may feel it, too, but it's only when they engage with the process, which may be just a few times in their lives. **So, the elegance of**

these new tech stacks is valued, but by those who are selling more than those who are buying. That's where demand for ease really lies. It is a "fail forward" moment.

While the word "failure" is used to describe the outcome of startups that thought their model would gain traction, I'd like to reframe that a bit for you. **It's not a failure to need humans. It's an important and hopeful lesson for the future.**

THE BIG TO-DO

Mapping the Universe of Experiences

The future of the industry lies in finding the right balance between technology and human labor. By understanding the strengths and limitations of both, we can create a system where AI supports humans, rather than trying to use it to replace them. This process will not only lead to better outcomes for consumers but also for the industry as a whole.

Use the spectrum shown in this chapter to plot the activities that are involved in the customer experience. Which of them might be misplaced? Which are falling short? What's working well? Why? *(x5)*.

CHAPTER SEVEN

COMPARE RESPONSIBLY

"Popular! / I'll help you be popular / You'll hang with the right cohorts / You'll be good at sports / Know the slang you've got to know / So, let's start / Cause you've got an awfully long way to go!"

–WICKED,
"Popular," 2003

One of the most notable, often joked about, elements of the "sold, not bought" category (negative demand category) is how socially unpopular it can make people feel. Consider the way you answer the question, "How did you get into this business?"

Many people I know would answer, "Quite by accident," or something similar. Me, too. I think the only people who don't get into the industry by accident are actuaries. *(Alright, hold your actuary jokes. I know many actuaries with personalities, and so, I don't laugh anymore at the stereotype. I will say, though, that I think they might be lazy. If you're a math major sitting in college and looking at an alphabetical list of professions that you could potentially pursue, you'll see actuary and say, "Okay, that'll do.")*

As a consequence to this feeling of unpopularity, I've noticed an underlying desire to become more like the "popular" industries. Wealth management is probably first on the list because it's a close adjacency to life insurance. While it's definitely sexier, it's really an unfair comparison for reasons you'll see later in this chapter. In addition, this comparison, and subsequent move for many in the industry into the wealth space, has created a void in the life insurance sphere. Many companies are exiting the life insurance business because wealth management is more lucrative and seemingly more relevant when you look at the demographics of existing customers. But the need for life insurance didn't go away, did it?

Beyond wealth management, however, I've also heard deeply ingrained desires of high-ranking executives to be more like the fashionable brands that have emerged as the powerhouses of today. It's like they want to wave a magic wand, much like Glinda the good witch in the *Wizard of Oz* and *Wicked*, and just be that popular. It has led to big investments with the promise not just of growth and sales, but also of shedding the feeling of unpopularity. Think of how the "nerds" like Bill Gates, Steve Wozniak, and Elon Musk got revenge on the cool football players and cheerleaders who may have teased them as kids. Instead of the prize being the ability to pick up hot chicks, for this industry, it's being liked by millenials and Gen Z! Any Insurtech startup that can promise a sizeable, youth-based audience would generate a big check. Unfortunately, without understanding all the dynamics of the negative demand category, many of these hip and cool new brands didn't make it while others pivoted.

APPLES AND ORANGES

Comparing apples and oranges can be a rabbit hole from which you'll never recover. Sure, they are both fruits, and both contain some kind of natural sugar, but they are still not the same. Still, people get so up in arms at the very thought of comparing an apple to an orange. Then, they always favor the apple.

In today's competitive business world, innovators are encouraged to look at successful businesses and ask, "Why can't we be more like them?"

This desire to emulate success can be powerful, but it can also be misleading, especially when comparisons are made between fundamentally different categories. Life insurance is often unfairly compared to other forms of insurance, banking, or even e-commerce giants like Amazon. However, these comparisons can distort our understanding of the unique and potentially unchangeable dynamics in the life insurance industry and misguide efforts to improve it.

UNFAIR COMPARISONS: THE PITFALLS OF TRYING TO BE SOMETHING YOU'RE NOT

Comparing life insurance to property and casualty insurance, health insurance, or even forms of banking seem reasonable at first glance. After all, these industries involve financial products, protection against risk, and the management of customer relationships. However, these comparisons fall short when we dig deeper into the nuances of each category.

Property and casualty insurance, for instance, deals with insurable risks that are often mandated by law—like auto insurance—where the demand is **built-in.** Creating demand isn't necessary, as the demand is attached to owning the car. Health insurance, similarly, has a strong pull, as medical expenses can be life-altering, and many individuals require insurance to avoid financial ruin in case of emergencies. When the Affordable Care Act came into place, it trained people into believing that health insurance was mandatory. *(Even though it technically isn't anymore.)* In contrast, life insurance is often seen as optional, and the demand is not as immediate or required by law. This fundamental difference in demand dynamics, therefore, makes it an unfair comparison to these other forms of insurance.

Comparing life insurance to banking is also misleading. While both banking and life insurance involve financial aspects, banking operates in a pull-demand environment. People actively seek out banks for loans, mortgages, and investment products because they have an immediate need for whatever that financial instrument is attached to (e.g. a house). By trying to compare life insurance to these other industries, we risk setting unrealistic expectations for what the industry can achieve. Instead, we should focus on making comparisons that acknowledge the unique challenges and opportunities within the life insurance industry.

It's tempting to wish that, by simply putting the right message out there, life insurance could suddenly become a product that people actively desire, one that they love to talk about at parties and eagerly recommend to friends. However, this fantasy is dangerously misleading.

PUSH VS. PULL MARKETING: THE ROLE OF ADVERTISING

As noted in Chapter Three, there's a sharp distinction between the types of marketing used in a demand category versus a negative demand category. Advertising plays a more prominent role in pull marketing than it does in push. Push marketing is the type that incentivizes the sellers to sell. The seller is like the "customer." Many arguments over the years have happened because of defining the customer as a seller or someone in the distribution chain. The objective in push marketing is to help the seller be better at their job, grow their sales, make more money, and in many cases, make them feel good about themselves in some way–i.e. rewards, recognition, etc. So, the activity is from the top down.

Pull, on the other hand, is when advertising messages and incentives are directed at the end buyer, the person who pays the money. The consumer receives the message and then just buys the product. The feelings that drive the desire to buy are not always logical and rational. There's a broad spectrum of them, in fact. If someone seeks out a shoe store or shoe website because there are holes in their favorite $50 Keds, that's one type of desire. Then, there are very different reasons people might spend $1,200 on a pair of red-bottomed Christian Louboutin shoes *(which really hurt, by the way, but they look amazing)*. There really isn't a two-way exchange needed for these products to be bought. The demand for those shoes already exists. People have likely seen ads for them everywhere already. The ad does its job–you don't need to ask someone, "Do you think these shoes will make me more attractive?" or "Will these shoes make me more desirable?" Ads alone, plus observing others who bought them, can drive the decision without people needing much of a conversation beforehand, much less a flip over an invisible wall.

Life insurance marketing isn't like *Madmen* marketing. As much as we'd love it to have that afternoon bourbon drinking glamor, catchy slogans don't do enough. They might be good for keeping a brand in someone's head *(like "Liberty Bibberty" or "We are Farmers, bum baddum bumm bumm")*, but alone, they don't sell a negative demand product. However, had there been some kind of two-way exchange prior to seeing the ad, it may provide the nudge needed to take action *(assuming it's easy and nothing screws it up)*.

As a digression, a fascinating story I learned during my time at Prudential was that their very memorable campaign from the 1970s, "Get a Piece of the Rock," only ran for a year and a half. It felt like an entrenched part of my childhood, and everyone born before 1980 seems to remember it. But you know why? It wasn't because of the TV ads. It was their 30,000 agents who took that message out to the public for years after the ads were created. Of course, they don't have nearly that many agents now, but it's very interesting to see how a pull campaign turned into a push one. It's also important to keep in mind that during those times, there were far fewer channels for receiving those messages, and the individual agent had the loudest voice for doing so.

THE INSURTECH REVOLUTION: A NEW PLAYER ON THE FIELD

In recent years, we've seen the rise of Insurtech, which, as you may recall, are companies that aim to bridge the gap between the old, traditional insurance models and modern technology. But now, there is a new kid in town who is out there to bridge the gap between push and pull marketing techniques, leveraging the three assets we did not have before:

1. Modern Technology
2. Young, hip, and cause-driven, millennial employees
3. Cool company names that smash two words together, remove vowels, misspell stuff, or use words that have only a distant connection with the service being offered. Just like the way rock bands and clothing brands are named.

These companies aim to make life insurance seem more accessible by appearing more in line with the lifestyle of younger generations. However, even they face the same fundamental challenges as traditional insurers: creating demand in a negative demand category. That's where the art of working together comes into play. The new technology, look, and feel is definitely more relevant and forward thinking. And then, the wisdom of the traditional insurance company is still very valuable and important.

ACCERN
Adjoint
air doctor
AKUR8
anorak
Atidot
AVENTUS
AXIOM
bambi
Bdeo
Visual Intelligence
Betterview
BEWICA
BEYONDMINDS
Blink Parametric
BOLD PENGUIN
DOMAPP
breathe
BRIISK
By Miles.
OMNISCIENCE
omni:us
Pentation Analytics
PLANCK
Praedicat
PremFina
QOMPLX:
quantiphi
REIN
Relay
RTHG
RIGHTINDEM
CAMBRIDGE MOBILE TELEMATICS
CCS
Cheche Tech
CHISEL AI
claimspace
Cobertoo
Collective
CURACEL
CyberCube
Cytora
dacadoo

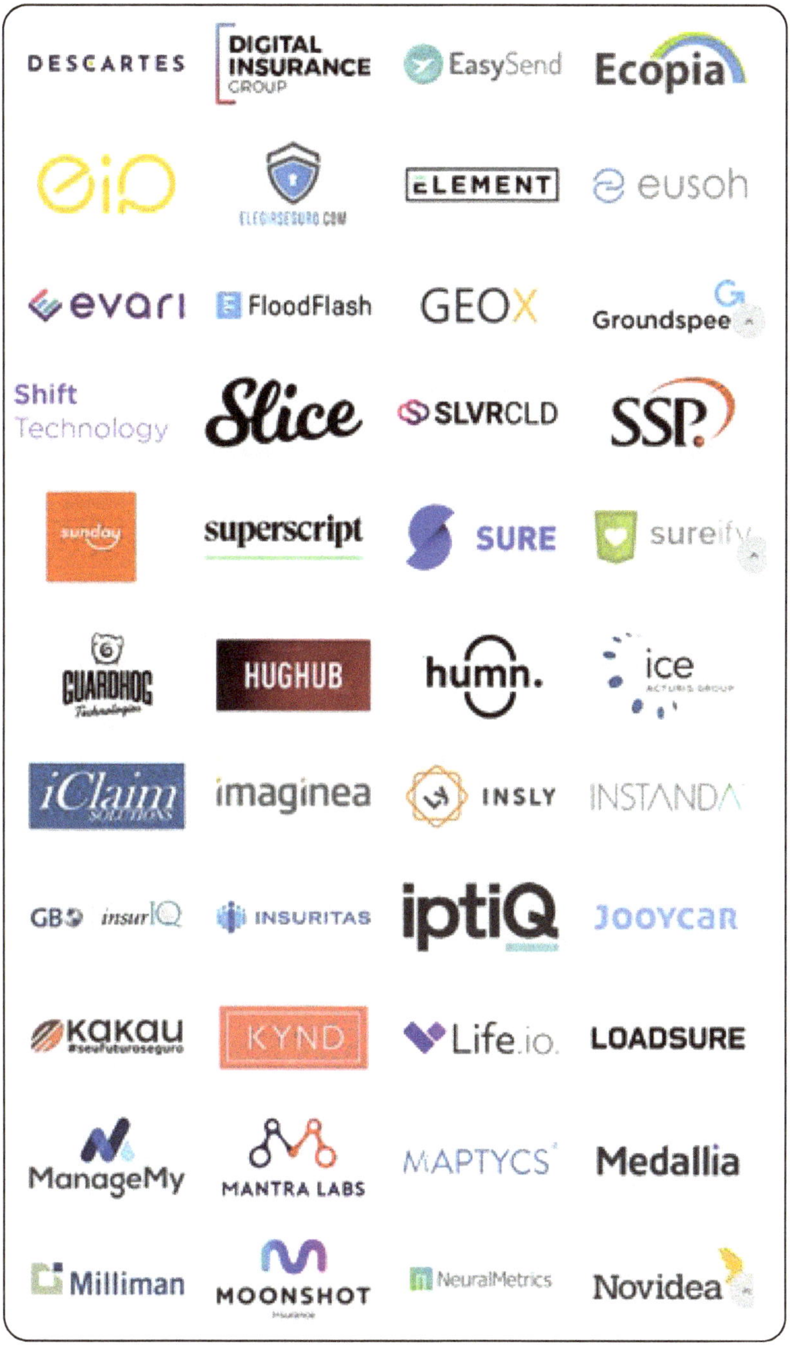

Figure 23: Insurtech brand names in 2020.

The collaboration between traditional life insurance companies and Insurtech startups can be likened to the unlikely partnership between David Bowie and Bing Crosby when they sang "Peace on Earth / The Little Drummer Boy." On the surface, these men represented different generations and styles, but together, they created something timeless. In the same way, the fusion of old insurance capital and new tech energy has the potential to reshape the industry—but only if both sides respect the unique challenges the life insurance industry presents and make fair comparisons to guide their strategies. *(Note that I think it would be really cool if Lin Manuel Miranda would write a hip-hop/rap third part to "Peace on Earth / The Little Drummer Boy" and bring it to a new generation. But I digress.)*

ATTRIBUTES OF FAIR COMPARISONS: A FRAMEWORK FOR MORE EFFECTIVE PROBLEM FRAMING

Now let's dive a little deeper into what comparisons are more fair. Keep in mind as you read this section that we are looking for singular attributes and not trying to assert that any profession or industry is "just like" that of life insurance. The objective is to open our minds to learning something new. Get curious, without defensiveness or a specific agenda.

NUANCE 17: Recipes for Fairness

Think about the TSA at the airport. The security measures they make you go through are often frustrating and unpleasant. People get upset with them because these procedures seem like obstacles when trying to get where you want to go. Tensions rise, especially when you're running late for a flight, and it's easy to get angry at TSA agents when they say, "Sorry, we need to scan you." But their job is about protection—just like life insurance.

The life insurance industry may not love this comparison, as it's important to elevate the profession's status. However, this little nuance is so similar. What can we learn from it? Have we ever asked high-ranking TSA officials how they handle those dynamics and tensions? I've seen signs at the airport that tell you the magnitude of a fine that you'll get if you threaten a TSA agent. I suspect that parallel may not be a fruitful one for us to emulate, as it's rooted in punishment. But then, more recently, I have seen signage that gives interesting facts about how many TSA agents are former military. In an instant, that kind of knowledge could transform the public's feeling of resentment to one of being grateful. Hmm.

Too often, insurance agents get compared to used car salesmen, which isn't a fair comparison, either, in my opinion. Cars are demand products. The common reason these two are often compared is because they are perceived to use pushy sales tactics. However, I have a nuanced hypothesis that the parallel with used cars is that they can have problems hidden under a mask of automotive complexity that only a mechanic can fully understand. Maybe that's the real driver of the perception and the comparison. It's the idea of getting into something that may backfire on you later because you're not knowledgeable enough to fully evaluate it. Pop culture has made it easy for the general public to latch onto the imagery of the cigar-smoking, pushy, sleazy deal-making salesman, which people still remember today, but I don't think that's how modern-day car salesmen look, either. With innovations like Car Facts, Carvana, etc., the old-fashioned negotiation smack-down is completely different now. This evolution is an example of a nuance that we need to extract and distinguish. Specifically, is it the pushy sales tactics that are truly the reason for the comparison, or is it the hidden "gotcha" that people are more worried about? Whatever it is, let's reframe the problem correctly, so we can fix it.

In Chapter Four, we discussed the imperative of the two-way exchange. Can you think of any other industries that are similar in that way? Up until recently, I might have been hard pressed to think of one. But a couple of years ago, I met a woman named Nancy, who I served with on the board of a fraternal benefit society. She read my book, *Flirting with the Uninterested*, in an effort to get to know me better *(which I deeply appreciate)*. However, when she told me that she did so, I was expecting her to say it didn't really make sense or apply to her, because she's not from the insurance industry. What I learned is that she found it very relevant. Why? Because she is a powerhouse in the field of charity fundraising. She totally related to the "sold, not bought" concept. Think about it. While people might make small donations to charities in a fairly friction-free way—such as rounding up, which is a brilliant idea—when it comes to getting large donations, there's *definitely* a need for a two-way exchange. You can't just ask for donations. You have to make a case for it, follow up, put up with rejection, etc.

If we are still committed to innovation in the life insurance industry, perhaps we should start with fairer comparisons. Instead of seeking inspiration just from the glamorous pull-oriented industries, maybe we can learn from those that may be on a similar playing field, like charities. Here are some attributes that can guide us on how to make fairer comparisons:

A GUIDE TO FAIRER COMPARISONS

Scan the QR code to view or download

ATTRIBUTE	INDUSTRY OR PRODUCT														
	Life Insurance	Organized Charity	Weight Loss Programs	TSA	AirBnB or Uber	Pre-Arranged Funeral	Will or Trust	Higher Education	Orthodontics	Sanitation/ Sewage	AARP/ Membership Groups	Mutual Fund/ Stocks	401k	Auto or Home Ins	Deep Cleaning Services (dryer ducts, etc.)
Negative vs Positive Emotions	●	●	◐	●	○	●	●	○	●	◐	○	○	○	●	●
Optional vs Mandatory	●	●	●	○	●	●	●	●	●	●	●	●	●	○	●
Wicked Problem?	●	●	●	●	○	○	○	○	○	○	○	○	●	○	○
Long Term Payoff vs Immediate Gratification	●	●	●	●	○	●	●	●	●	○	○	●	●	●	○
Not Ultimately for the Person Who Buys It/ Uses It	●	●	○	◐	○	●	●	●	●	○	○	○	○	◐	○
Planning Ahead / Preventing Something Bad	●	◐	●	●	○	●	●	○	◐	○	○	●	●	●	●
Sharing / Pooling is involved	●	●	○	●	●	○	○	○	○	●	●	●	●	●	○
Multiple Currencies Required (not just money)	●	○	●	○	○	○	○	●	○	○	●	○	○	●	○
Two-Way Exchange Is Most Helpful in Taking Action (Push vs. Pull)	●	●	●	◐	○	●	○	○	●	○	○	●	○	○	●
Heavenly Virtues Vs "Deadly Sin" Sale	●	●	◐	●	○	●	●	●	○	●	○	◐	●	●	●
Paying Money For Money	●	●	○	○	○	●	○	○	○	○	○	●	●	●	○
Easy to Take For Granted	●	○	○	●	○	○	○	●	○	●	○	○	●	●	●
Feels Clunky/ Complicated	●	○	○	●	○	○	●	●	●	○	○	●	●	○	○
Low Level of Engagement	●	○	○	○	○	●	●	○	○	○	○	○	○	○	●

EACH ATTRIBUTE IS DESCRIBED WITH EXAMPLES STARTING ON THE NEXT PAGE.

Use the QR code above to view or download the chart in a readable form.

● Means the attribute is true for that industry or product.

◐ Means it is partly or sometimes true.

○ Means it is generally untrue.

1. **Negative Emotions vs. Positive Emotions:** Life insurance is frequently associated with negative, off-putting emotions—fear of death, loss, and financial insecurity. Fair comparisons should be made with other products or services that also operate in a negative-emotion context, such as pre-arranged funerals, wills and trusts, nursing home care, collection agencies, and charities that help those in situations where they are victims of such losses. One of my favorite—or least favorite, in reality—examples is the ASPCA. When I see shivering dogs and starving cats while Willie Nelson is singing "You Were Always on My Mind," I get so upset that I have to turn off the TV. And no, I don't donate, either, because it's just that upsetting to me. *(But then again, I am hypersensitive to such things. It must work for someone!)*

2. **Optional vs. Mandatory:** Unlike health insurance, which was once mandated by law, life insurance is not. Comparisons should take into account whether a product is mandatory or voluntary, as this difference significantly affects consumer behavior and demand. So, if the comparing category is mandatory, like auto and home insurance, it might not be that helpful other than as a point of reference.

3. **Wicked vs. Tame Problem:** Is the industry you're comparing to also dealing with a wicked problem, as explained in Chapter Three? Or is it really a tame problem? Complexity is present in both, but predictable outcomes and replication are only true with tame problems.

4. **Long-Term "Payoff" vs. Immediate Gratification:** Life insurance benefits are not seen for a long time, hopefully, and any cash value that might accumulate won't do so for years. Fair comparisons should focus on products that require upfront investment for something in the future. For example, consider other investments that we make just knowing it's the right thing to do like gym memberships or weight loss, but it requires patience to get to the ultimate outcome.

5. **Who's It for?** Is the product you're comparing it to meant for the person who buys or pays for it? Or does it benefit someone else? *(Like braces or higher education for your kid.)*

6. **Preventing Something Bad vs. Inviting Something Good:** Life insurance prevents the destitution and financial loss from the death of someone whose income is relied upon by others. You have to get it before you need it. Other products and services with this characteristic include preventative healthcare, dryer duct/gutter cleaning, pest control, cyber security training, and the Transportation Security Administration (TSA).

7. **Sharing Model vs. One-on-One:** Life insurance and other kinds of insurance leverages the power of many to create the outcome. Pooling resources is the industry vernacular for describing this dynamic. If the product or services is an outgrowth of some kind of sharing model, such as pension plans, utilities, and anything else that shares resources and also has an element of basic human needs—as opposed to sharing a vacation home on Airbnb—it's a fairer comparison.

8. **Multiple Currencies vs. Just Money:** Life insurance is unique in that it's not something you can just "get" with money anytime you want it. You pay for it with multiple currencies. Money is one type, but there's also health and age that play huge factors. These two characteristics may determine how much the policy will cost, or even if you can get it at all. So, a fairer comparison might be a membership group that has an age restriction like AARP or YPO. Perhaps another similar comparison could be preferred airline status, which you can't really just buy into, either. You have to fly the miles as well.

9. **Two-Way Exchange vs. One-Way Exchange:** We identified the imperative of the two-way exchange and how important it is to flip someone over that invisible wall. The best example I can give here, as explained above, is the charity fundraising field. Perhaps even political campaigns can be a source of learning, particularly in situations like we are in now with the last several races being very close. Since there's been a great sense of division, it has led to people having to "strong arm" others to get specific votes. Hmm. Sounds a lot like judo flipping someone over a wall.

10. **Heavenly Virtues vs. Deadly Sins:** Now, here's a comparison that is sure to be controversy free *(LOL!)* I had the pleasure of getting to know Ariel Pfeffer, an entrepreneur and life coach from Uruguay, who started working with a life insurance industry professional I know named Jeremy Reinbolt in Canada. They are teaming up to innovate in this space. During that conversation,

Ariel noted that for successful sales of anything, you must appeal to one or more of the seven deadly sins—which for reference are pride, greed, lust, envy, gluttony, wrath, and sloth. He emphasized greed, pride, sloth, and envy. For example, to appeal to greed, one might offer discounts or suggest they are getting a great deal. To appeal to envy, one might attempt to show how what they have gotten is exclusive and not available to just anyone.

Inspired by this idea, because it was something I never really heard of before, I dug into it a little more *(specifically by going down the rabbit hole that is Wikipedia)*. I also started clicking on the seven heavenly virtues, which are chastity, temperance, charity, diligence, kindness, patience, and humility. What I noticed is that it's a whole lot easier to see the purpose of life insurance inside the virtues versus the sins. But if sin sells, then therein lies an unfair comparison because it's really hard to flip life insurance into a "sinful" sale in a way that isn't forced or feels exploitative. While I don't believe I need to go to confession for owning a pair of stiletto heels *(Or do I?)*, let's face it, sin is what sells a pair of Christian Louboutin shoes. So, what does that mean for a fairer comparison? What are the products and services that align with the seven virtues? Organized charity comes up again here, as well as weight loss/appetite control products, Alcoholics Anonymous, and maybe even meditation, mindfulness services, and deep cleaning services.

11. **Paying Money for Money:** As stated in Chapter Two, some "products" or uses of money are to receive money back eventually or to turn it into money for someone else. Is whatever you are comparing to similar in that way?

12. **Easy to Take for Granted:** As also stated previously, things like utilities, which feel like they should just be part of being human, make for better comparisons.

13. **Feels Clunky or Complicated to Get:** This issue is where a lot of industry energy has been directed toward, which is helpful. Continued progress comes from learning from other categories that have the same dynamics and may have solved them.

14. **Low Engagement Over Time:** In *Flirting with the Uninterested*, we identified life insurance as a low engagement category. This fact is generally still true, except that some companies have wisely been experimenting and innovating around health and fitness engagement as part of the package. Apart from that, if it's a "buy it and put it in the drawer" product, it's probably a fair comparison.

By using these attributes to guide comparisons, life insurance companies may be able to learn new things and identify new nuances that can better help propel the mission forward in a more effective way.

In addition, we need to acknowledge that life insurance and the reasoning behind getting it has changed over the years. As society progresses, the risks that life insurance protects against have changed. Workplace safety standards have improved dramatically, and fewer people are employed in dangerous jobs like coal mining or chemical manufacturing. With these shifts, the financial risks associated with premature death have lessened. That doesn't mean life insurance is any less important, because after all, the "if" is so much more important than the likelihood. In other words, just because the probability is lower, it doesn't mean the consequences aren't severe when it actually does happen. However, it does mean that our expectations need to evolve around how to continually be relevant.

THE BIG TO-DO

Finding the Right Inspiration for Your Teams

Ultimately, the goal of making responsible comparisons is to inspire innovation and improvement within the life insurance industry. By finding the right inspiration—whether it's from utilities, preventive healthcare, the TSA, or charity fundraising—companies can better align their efforts with the realities of their offerings.

You may ask, "How do you effectively use this inspiration?" Well, if you've read this far, I will share a secret with you. You ask people in those professions for help!

In my decade-plus working at Maddock Douglas, by far the phrase that we use that resonates most with our innovation clients is, "**You can't read the label when you're sitting inside the jar.**"

Everyone who is doing a job for more than a year or so is inside a jar. That means you are an expert at what you know, including the pitfalls, the mistakes, the "oh, that'll never work, we tried it, and it failed" syndrome. Take heart, there's a way out of the jar, and that's parallel universes. Look for industries that have solved or dealt with similar problems and challenges. Be really thoughtful about how you define those problems first. Then, find professionals in your network who come from those industries. Reach out and ask them for an hour or so of time. You could offer to pay them $150 *(LOL!)* just to sit and talk with you. But oftentimes, people will do it for free because it's so much more fun to work on someone else's problem than your own. We do so routinely as part of our discovery process for generating insights and ideas. At Maddock Douglas, it is what we call our Global Expert Network. We can find just about anyone we need from it. But it's not rocket science; it's simply a very good habit that people don't typically think of doing before they embark on creative problem solving.

As the industry evolves, the key to success will be balancing tradition with innovation, all while making fair comparisons that guide responsible growth. By understanding what life insurance truly is—and what it isn't—companies can move forward with strategies that make sense, rather than chasing unrealistic comparisons that only lead to disappointment.

In the end, the most successful life insurance companies will be those that embrace their unique role, purpose, and the characteristics that go along with it, without trying to be something they're not.

CHAPTER EIGHT

A PORTFOLIO OF PURPOSE

"Some day, yeah / We'll get it together, and we'll get it all done / Some day / When your head is much lighter / Some day, yeah / We'll walk in the rays of a beautiful sun / Some day / When the world is much brighter."

–THE FIVE STAIRSTEPS,
"Ooh Child," 1970

We keep talking about what we need to do better, but who is actually learning from what we have not done right in the past? Are we all just waiting to have a good nap after the big conference where we said, "Yea! Let's do this!" Or maybe we don't know what to do differently?

Sometimes, it seems as if no one wants to work anymore—when it comes to selling life insurance, at least. *(Said the old lady to the young whippersnapper!)*

The process of convincing others to mitigate risk for their loved ones is a challenging task, one that comes with cold calls, mistakes, and the need to channel sincerity and authenticity into every conversation, even on the days when you don't feel like it. Have you ever tried being authentic with everyone you meet, from the grocer to the mail carrier? It can be exhausting. As a result, many new agents burn out, quit, or fail, which is the dilemma when we are looking to close the protection gap and grow the industry's reach.

The problem with creating organic growth, whether it be insuring more people, recruiting more agents, or using another attractive metric, is that it often leads to navel-gazing to figure out what went wrong. In the life insurance industry, self-reflection is vital, but self-flagellation—the constant berating of ourselves for our perceived failures—often masquerades as progress.

SELF-FLAGELLATION ISN'T PROGRESS

It can feel productive to acknowledge our shortcomings and criticize our collective performance, especially in public forums or industry panels. Picture a group of high-ranking life insurance executives on a stage in directors' chairs with their feet awkwardly trying to rest on the bars below. They are looking at each other, trying to figure out who is supposed to go first. Then, the moderator asks the panel what they think is the reason for flat sales or the growing protection gap, which is the difference between how much life insurance people should have and what they actually have. One CEO boldly falls on the sword and states, "We are doing a terrible job of ____________________." You can fill in the blank with "educating people," "making the experience of buying easy," "reaching the middle market," "leveraging technology," etc., etc. The crowd cheers. The brave CEO feels good for that moment.

However, while self-flagellation might generate conversation, it is not enough to make the substantive changes we need to create real impact. *(It might even be a sin, LOL!)* This chapter will explore the need to shift our energy from self-criticism to purposeful problem definition and define what changes are necessary to attract more talent and improve the industry. Plus, this chapter will cover how to cultivate a portfolio of innovations that can help the industry evolve in a meaningful way.

Despite being well-applauded by our peers, self-flagellation hasn't led to applause from prospective customers. In fact, many consumers don't even sense the problems we feel at all. If we were to put a headline in the newspaper about the ever-growing life insurance protection gap, most consumers would just turn the page. However, when the industry professionals see it, all hell breaks loose.

The industry's collective effort to close the gap between its intentions and consumer perceptions is worthy, but the conversation often overlooks critical nuances. Consumers don't just misunderstand life insurance; they respond to it based on deeply ingrained behaviors, biases, and emotional triggers. Simply declaring that we need to do better won't address these complexities.

Progress comes from nuanced, thoughtful actions that address the root causes of consumer hesitation and disengagement. Human-centered design thinking is the critical skill that's underdeveloped. It's how the best customer experiences are created, but more importantly, it's how progress on wicked problems is made. We will cover such concepts later on in the chapter.

SERENITY NOW!

"Grant me the serenity to accept the things I cannot change, the courage to change the things I can, and the wisdom to know the difference." As clichéd as it may sound, this serenity prayer has a great deal of wisdom to be extracted. I think those in the life insurance industry could benefit from this wisdom and apply it to their work strategies when it comes to generating sales, recruiting new agents, and progressing towards a better future for everyone involved.

In Chapter Six, we talked about getting the division of labor right. There's a spectrum of things that humans can do really well and that the bots can do really well. Let's use that as a guide for how we envision a portfolio of ideas, solutions, and experiments to learn and progress.

WHAT CAN'T WE CHANGE? A STARTER LIST

Okay, let's get practical. If we define what's changeable and what's not, even if we might be wrong about some of it, that's a great starting point to "serenity" based on what we discussed in previous chapters. Below is a list of invariable facts that those of us in the life insurance industry have to accept.

1. Humans will behave irrationally.
2. Life insurance is a negative demand product, generally speaking.
3. We need to have a two-way exchange to take action.

4. Humans are responsible for handling any irrational aspects. Tech can handle most, if not all, things rational.
5. Empathy is critical to handling all things irrational.
6. Pooling resources is the most important superpower of the industry.
7. There's no right way to do a wrong thing (intent).

What else seems like a "can't touch this" item? I am open to others, but let's start here. If these seven untouchables are true, then we may be able to impact just about anything else.

A WORD ABOUT THE COMPENSATION MODEL

It may be tempting to think that the compensation model should be on the list above. Currently, agents often receive large commissions upfront when a policy is sold, followed by much smaller amounts in subsequent years. We talked earlier about de-shaming the commission model, because there's alignment between where the hard work is and where the money is. However, maybe it's time to consider new dimensions to measure and reward success.

In the same 2020 study mentioned earlier about the post-pandemic future of the trusted advisor by Maddock Douglas, we tested the controversial topic of commission-based sales. Not just in this industry, but others as well. The upside is that there's a wide difference of opinion between how professionals versus the consuming public see this issue. The consumer is pressuring us to redesign it and base more of the compensation on some level of customer satisfaction rather than just closing a sale. How to do that, I don't have an answer.

However, I suspect that there are very few, if any at all, who are working hard on this idea. Why? Any changes to the compensation model would need to be carefully considered. The initial accomplishment of getting a client to purchase life insurance is substantial and should be rewarded, but the first company to move away from the current model will presumably lose the business they have today. So, there would have to be a parallel track where new people are brought into a new compensation model. There'd have to be enough patience to test, fail, and learn, as well as a commitment to seeing it through. I still think this task is worth pursuing, but who would have both the brains and the stomach to do it?

THE VALUE OF GUARDRAILS (CONSTRAINTS)

Let's talk about constraints for a moment. A misconception in the realm of innovation is that we need to be constraint-free to be the most creative. On the contrary, constraints foster creativity.

Here's a case in point. The following is obviously a true story, but I will describe it with the vision of the movie *Apollo 13*. If you're not familiar with the mission back in 1970, it involved sending astronauts into space with the goal of landing on the moon for the third time, but then, there was a problem with the craft. After something broke, carbon dioxide levels were rising and would have caused the astronauts to eventually pass out and die before they got back.

One of the astronauts, Jack Swigert, famously radioed to mission control and said "Houston, we have a problem." Kevin Bacon played this part in the 1995 film that was inspired by this mission. If you know the story, you know that it has a happy ending. They got back safely.

However, it was not by luck. It was through the engineers' and astronauts' excellence in defining and solving problems, understanding constraints, and applying massive creativity once those parameters were understood. It's such a great example of the power of these skills. Gives me chills every time I think about it.

The way it manifested in the dramatic film is that one of the engineers on the ground in Houston comes running into a conference room with a big box in his hands that contained all the items they had on the spacecraft and dumps it on the table. There are other engineers and experts in the room. He holds up a piece of pipe that's round and a machine part that's square. He then says, "We have to figure out a way to fit this into the hole for this, using nothing but that." And he points to the pile on the table.

Having to perform such a maneuver with a lack of resources was a huge constraint. With that said, the engineers were able to become super creative instead of spending valuable time contemplating infinite possibilities that may or may not have been discovered in time.

I firmly believe that our skills in defining the problems and constraints can get a lot better. It will require building new skills and developing disciplines that not all people are capable of developing, but each individual on your team probably has some skill that they *can* develop, and that can be leveraged for different things.

NUANCE 18: Not All Innovation Is Created Equally

If you or anyone in your company takes an attitude about innovation that sounds like, "I'll know it when I see it," please take a second to reflect.

Not all innovation is created equally. It's important to define innovation specifically so that everyone on your team knows what it means. My colleagues define it as the intersection between an unmet need in the market, an idea for meeting it, and the execution that makes it actually sell. However, there are different flavors of innovation, which are based on the dynamics of your capabilities, whether or not the market is really ready for the proposed change or solution, or if the need is an actual concern for the consumers.

In order to move the industry forward, though, we need to cultivate an innovation portfolio that includes various approaches to solving the challenges we face. Not every idea will succeed, but by embracing a range of innovation strategies, which include evolutionary, differentiation, fast fail, and revolutionary, we can push the industry toward meaningful progress. The innovation portfolio model that is described next was developed by Maddock Douglas. It was written about by one of our treasured partners, Gino Chirio, in the *Harvard Business Review* ("The 6 Ways to Grow a Company," 2018).

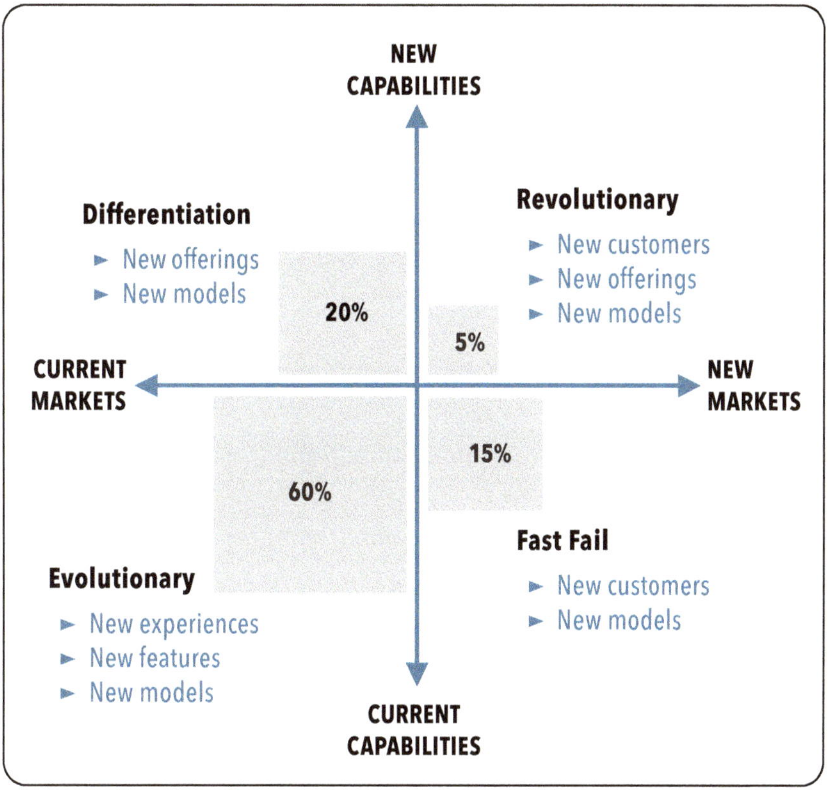

Figure 24: The Innovation Portfolio, Maddock Douglas, Inc.

EVOLUTIONARY INNOVATION

Evolutionary innovation involves making incremental improvements to existing processes and products. This strategy might include refining the sales process, enhancing customer service, or improving the way we communicate with clients. While these changes may seem small, they can have a significant impact over time. Evolutionary innovation allows the industry to adapt and improve without the risk of overhauling everything at once. Too much change too soon could produce just as many new issues as it solves.

For example, many companies are exploring ways to use AI to support agents in their daily tasks, such as automating administrative work, streamlining underwriting, or helping with routine client communication. These incremental changes free up agents to focus on what they do best—building relationships and providing personalized advice. However, just as we've already covered, AI doesn't completely replace the agents. Technology still can't provide the same level of care and genuine connection that humans can. Evolutionary innovation could also include empathy training and training that helps agents manage fear.

These innovations are things we can easily wrap our heads around now, and we can see a clear path to execution, with results available in the (relatively) short-term.

DIFFERENTIATION INNOVATION

Differentiation innovation involves finding new ways to stand out in a crowded marketplace. In the life insurance industry, that could mean offering unique products or services that set a company apart from its competitors. For example, some companies are experimenting with wellness programs that incentivize healthy behaviors, rewarding clients with discounts or benefits for maintaining good health. Others are going all in on their technology platforms that are designed to perfect the process of how life insurance is underwritten and serviced.

Others still may commit to creating a business model that harnesses the two-way exchange in a new way, thereby improving the 10-3-1 ratio.

Here, the key is to focus on anything that you know the market is going to want, but it is somehow daunting to do it well. Once these innovations are developed, they must be fiercely protected; otherwise, others will copy it.

These are innovations that we can also wrap our heads around now, but there's something really difficult about doing it effectively. Typically, it's a complex, yet tame problem.

FAST FAIL INNOVATION

Fast fail innovation is about experimenting with new ideas quickly and learning from any failures that may occur. While failure and failing forward, which means learning from failures and using them as stepping stones toward success, is important for all four types of innovation, this approach encourages failing quickly. It's about trying out new concepts on a small scale, evaluating the results, and either pivoting in a new direction or abandoning the idea entirely based on the documented outcomes. Fast fail innovation allows for rapid iteration and prevents companies from sinking too much time and money into ideas that don't work.

For example, a company might pilot a new compensation model in a new market with a new type of agent to keep it away from the core business and not upset the current "cash cow." If the idea doesn't show promise, the company can quickly adjust its strategy without committing to a full-scale rollout. Fast fail innovation requires a willingness to take risks and embrace failure as part of the learning process and commit to a well-defined learning agenda.

This type of innovation is where we can envision something working, but we are not sure what the true hook is and need to experiment to find out.

REVOLUTIONARY INNOVATION

Revolutionary innovation involves bold, transformative ideas that have the potential to disrupt the industry or create new branches of it. This type of innovation is riskier, but it can also yield the greatest rewards. Revolutionary innovation might involve completely rethinking what we do with the constraints that we know we have. It requires defining what business we have the right to be in, not just the one we are in now.

Another way to think about revolutionary innovation is to imagine new uses for our core capabilities, aiming toward new methods that are relevant or emerging. So, it might not be life insurance at all, but rather, it might be the next big thing that leverages the same superpowers. *(See Chapter Ten for a wild example.)*

These innovations are the ones that few people can conceive fully. There's a hunch that something is possible, but we don't know yet what it is until more information becomes clear.

THE BIG TO-DO

Failing Forward Starts with Better Expectations for Learning (Not Lip Service)

When it comes to innovation, there's often talk about the importance of failing forward. However, failing forward must be more than just a buzzword. It requires a cultural shift that encourages experimentation, calculated risks, and viewing failure as a necessary part of innovation. *(BTW, failure is present in every part of the portfolio, not just the fast fail quadrant!)*

Accepting failure may sound and, for many in the industry, is seen as something to be avoided at all costs. The fear of failure, however, can stifle creativity and prevent companies from taking the bold steps needed to drive real change. To truly embrace failing forward, the industry needs to create an environment where failure is seen as an opportunity to learn, not as a career-ending mistake.

Startups in the Insurtech space have already embraced this mindset. They experiment with new ideas, launch products quickly, and pivot when things don't go as planned. Traditional life insurance companies can learn from this approach by fostering a culture that values innovation and views failure as a vital part of the process.

Embracing a fail-forward mentality also means recognizing that not every innovation will succeed—and that's okay. The key is to **learn from each failure** and use that knowledge to improve future efforts. By building a portfolio of purposeful innovations, the life insurance industry can continue to evolve and better meet the needs of consumers. Failure should not be "fatal" to a job unless the same mistake is made over and over with no learning.

A skillset inside of failing forward and human-centered design is **creative problem solving.** It starts with examining and defining the problem, which is referred to as **problem reframing**. Einstein would describe it as, "If I have an hour to solve a problem, I will spend fifty-five minutes defining the problem and then five minutes solving it." As everyone knows, Einstein was no dummy! This mindset is the crux of innovation. *(Not to mention his zen-like patience for observation and experimentation!)*

When we fail, it's often not because our solution was bad. Instead, it is because our problem was not articulated correctly. The classic example is, "Do you need a drill or a hole?" If you need a hole, then a drill is only one way to solve the problem. In the context of life insurance, what problem are we really solving? I hear over and over that "we just have to get the message out there." I completely disagree with this definition of the problem. It's much more nuanced than that, as described in the eighteen nuances that precede this chapter, and the ones that follow.

For instance, back in my days at a life insurance carrier, I was given the task to thwart Suzie Orman's view of whole life insurance. The "obvious" answer to all involved was some kind of advertising campaign or promotional tackle-fest, which would have cost millions. Furthermore, it probably would have failed with the strength of Suzie's voice and the lackluster image of the industry. But after meticulous problem reframing, we learned that a big portion of the problem was not Suzie making consumers feel bad about whole life insurance; it was her making other professionals, such as accountants, think it was bad. As a result, they were unwinding sales in progress. That nuance led to the idea of "Life Insurance as an Asset Class," a white paper authored by my friend and respected colleague, Dick Weber. He, after we reframed the problem in a new way, helped us design the proof that whole life is a strategy that can mitigate investment risk and create healthier, more predictable portfolios for people with assets to invest. The resulting white paper and education for CPAs instilled greater confidence in the advisors working on these issues. *(And it was also copied by several companies in the US and Canada in the following ten years!)*

The finer point we need to focus on now is to make sure that we are really paying attention to the lessons we are learning, not just saying, "That didn't work." We need to get much more precise about learning agendas, problem definition, and nuances of insight. Every experiment should have a learning agenda. Every failure should have a set of lessons that tells you something you did not know before. If your team has not generated that learning, then you've either repeated a past mistake, have "failed backward," or you have not examined what happened deeply enough.

In conclusion, the life insurance industry faces unique challenges, but by focusing on what we can change, embracing innovation, and fostering a culture that values learning from failure, we can move toward a future where success generates more applause than self-flagellation.

CHAPTER NINE

THE BLIND SPOTS

"Imagine there's no countries / It isn't hard to do / Nothing to kill or die for / And no religion, too."

–JOHN LENNON,

"Imagine," 1971

John Lennon had a unique ability to picture things that seemed unreasonable or impossible. So much so that he was criticized for things he observed and spoke about. His ability to see things others couldn't see and go on to speak about them was a factor in what drove his assassin's motives. What a damn shame.

John was an innovator, not just in music but with his ideas around how to solve the world's problems. It's easy to say things like, "Oh, that'll never happen," until it does. I know from my experience working in the life insurance industry, I've been critically called out as a "dreamer" in meetings where I have presented new ideas. But I'm not the only one.

Innovation is often driven by a keen awareness of the challenges and opportunities that lie ahead. However, there are always blind spots—those unseen, unanticipated disruptions that can turn an entire industry upside down. This chapter explores the nature of blind spots, using real-world examples and thought experiments to illustrate how we can recognize and address these hidden threats before they render us obsolete.

A CAR WASH IN BRAZIL: A CLASSIC STORY OF A BLIND SPOT

Blind spots are, by their very nature, difficult or impossible to see. They can arise from unexpected developments in adjacent industries, shifts in consumer behavior, or even technological advancements. To understand the nature of blind spots, let's begin with a seemingly unrelated story about a car wash in Brazil that I heard about during a presentation at a conference for the real estate industry.

In Brazil, car washes were a thriving business at one point. Proud of their cars, people ensured that their vehicles remained spotless. Over a decade, however, the owners of one particular car wash began to notice a steady decline in business. Sales dropped by half, and despite the country's continued love of cars, fewer people were bringing them in for a wash. The owners of the car wash were baffled.

It wasn't until they dug deeper that they realized the cause: advances in weather prediction technology. Weather forecasting had become so accurate that people knew exactly when it was going to rain, and as a result, they were only washing their cars on days when they were sure it wouldn't rain. Before, people had washed their cars whenever they felt they were dirty, which meant that business remained steady; now, they were timing it based on weather forecasts. The car wash owners had never considered that advancements in weather technology could impact their business, but this unforeseen shift in consumer behavior cut their sales in half.

This story highlights the core essence of blind spots: they are factors we don't even think to consider, yet they can have a profound impact on our business. In the life insurance industry, we need to be vigilant about identifying our own blind spots before they catch us off-guard.

METHUSELARITY: WHAT IF PEOPLE REALLY COULD LIVE (ALMOST) FOREVER?

What the heck? How'd we go from a car wash to here? Oh, well, let's roll with it!

One of the most provocative blind spots for the life insurance industry, in my opinion, is the concept of "Methuselarity," or the idea that people could live for an extended period of time, or even indefinitely, due to advancements in medicine and technology. The term, popularized by researcher Aubrey de Grey, refers to a point in time where medical science could halt or reverse the aging process, allowing people to live far longer than they do today.

If you've ever read the Bible, the book of Genesis tells the stories of men who lived to be more than 700 years old. While many people seem to think these tales have more to do with how people measured time, it could become something more tangible with modern science. At first glance, this notion may seem like science fiction. However, the rapid pace of technological advancement makes it conceivable that future generations could experience significant extensions in life expectancy. Ray Kurzweil, a prominent futurist, has described aging as a "solvable engineering problem" *(akin to a tame problem outlined in Chapter Three)* and suggested that we could soon reach a point where we'll add one year to our lifespan for every year we live. This concept, known as "escape velocity," could lead to a world where people live well beyond a hundred years, possibly even centuries.

If this scenario was to unfold, the implications for the life insurance industry would be profound. Traditional life insurance products, which are based on the assumption that everyone will eventually die within a certain timeframe, could become obsolete. If people lived for hundreds of years—or even indefinitely—how would the industry adapt? How would pricing, policy terms, and actuarial models evolve? The very foundation of life insurance could be called into question if such a drastic change were to occur. Even a variation on this theme, such as being able to predict when someone would die, also disrupts the tenets of probability as we know them today.

While this scenario may not happen for some time, if it does at all, it serves as a reminder that the future is unpredictable. The life insurance industry needs to be prepared for the possibility that advancements in longevity could fundamentally alter the market.

If you think this notion isn't possible, think again. *Star Trek* has been remarkably prescient in predicting several modern technologies, many of which have become integral parts of our daily lives. For instance, the communicators used in the original series are strikingly similar to today's smartphones, which enable global communication and access to vast amounts of information from a handheld device. Similarly, the PADDs (Personal Access Display Devices) featured in *Star Trek: The Next Generation* anticipated modern tablets' design and functionality, allowing users to perform various tasks on the go.

Another significant prediction was the concept of voice-activated interfaces, as seen in the LCARS (Library Computer Access/Retrieval System) in *The Next Generation*. This technology mirrors today's virtual assistants, such as Siri and Alexa, which allow users to interact with devices through verbal language commands. Additionally, the replicators from *Star Trek: Voyager*, which could create objects on demand, foreshadowed the development of 3D printing technology. This modern innovation now allows for the creation of complex structures, including medical implants, from digital designs. Lastly, the holodecks in the series introduced the idea of immersive virtual environments, a concept now partially realized through virtual reality (VR) technology, widely used in gaming, education, and training. You can't make some of this stuff up.

COSTLESS SOCIETY

Another potential blind spot is the concept of a "costless society." This idea suggests that as technology continues to advance, the cost of basic goods and services could decrease dramatically to the point where money itself may lose its value. While it might seem implausible in today's world of inflation and economic instability, the long-term trends in technology suggest that the cost of essential resources—food, water, shelter, and even energy—could continue to fall.

Take, for example, the advancements in renewable energy, 3D printing, and automation. These technologies have the potential to reduce the cost of production and distribution for a wide range of goods. In a world where the basic necessities of life are either free or nearly free, what role would money play? Furthermore, if people no longer needed to accumulate wealth to secure their future, what would happen to the life insurance industry, which is fundamentally about financial protection?

The implications of a costless society for life insurance are significant. If people no longer need money to ensure their survival, what would they insure? Would life insurance products need to shift focus away from financial protection and towards other forms of value, such as protecting access to scarce resources or guaranteeing rights to exclusive experiences?

Again, while this scenario may seem farfetched, the possibility of a world where money holds less value is worth considering. The industry needs to start thinking about how it would adapt to such a fundamental shift in societal priorities.

SEEING BLIND SPOTS: THE OXYMORON OF IT ALL

The challenge with blind spots is that, by definition, they are difficult to see. Asking someone to identify their blind spots is like asking a fish to see the water it swims in—it's nearly impossible. However, by embracing curiosity, exploring farfetched scenarios, and looking beyond our immediate industry, we can start to identify potential blind spots before they become existential threats. We can create solutions now, before the problems even fully present themselves.

NUANCE 19: What Do We Take for Granted?

To uncover these blind spots, we need to challenge our assumptions. What do we take for granted about our industry that may not hold true in the future? Are there developments in adjacent industries that could have a ripple effect on life insurance? Are there emerging technologies that could disrupt the way we do business? By asking these questions and encouraging creative and critical thinking skills in our agents, we can start to see the edges of our blind spots and prepare for the unexpected.

THE BIG TO-DO

Rally Your Crazies

Every organization needs people who think differently, those who can see beyond the status quo and imagine a future that doesn't yet exist. These "crazies" are often the ones who can identify blind spots that others may miss. They may propose ideas that seem outlandish at first, but in reality, they are essential to fostering innovation and staying ahead of disruption.

Identify those creative thinkers in your organization and give them a platform to share their ideas. Sometimes, these people are seen as odd or even off-putting. Encourage collaboration between them and more traditional thinkers to strike a balance between innovation and practicality.

To turn blind spots into revolutionary innovation, leaders in the life insurance industry need to create an environment where these "crazies" can thrive. That means encouraging experimentation, embracing failure, and being open to ideas that challenge the traditional way of doing things. It also means building a culture of continuous learning and curiosity, where people are encouraged to look beyond their immediate responsibilities and explore new possibilities for the industry's future. Here is a list of things you can ask your creative thinkers to do:

1. **Challenge Assumptions:** Regularly question the assumptions that underpin your business. What are you taking for granted that might not hold true in the future? Encourage your team to think critically and creatively about the industry's future.

2. **Explore Adjacent Industries:** Look beyond the life insurance industry for inspiration. What's happening in other sectors that could have a ripple effect on your business? Are there innovations in technology, healthcare, or finance that could disrupt life insurance as we know it?

3. **Embrace Provocative Ideas:** Don't dismiss ideas just because they seem farfetched. Encourage your team to explore provocative concepts like Methuselarity or a costless society, even if they seem unlikely. These thought experiments can help you identify potential blind spots and prepare for unexpected developments. What other ones can you think of?

4. **Foster a Culture of Experimentation:** Create an environment where experimentation is encouraged and failure is seen as a learning opportunity. Give your team the freedom to test new ideas in small, contained ways, even if they don't align with traditional business practices.

5. **Look for Early Warning Signs:** Pay attention to developments on the fringes of your industry. What are the early warning signs that a disruptive innovation might be on the horizon? By staying attuned to these signals, you can start preparing for potential blind spots before they become major issues. Make this task someone's full-time job, and don't fire them when you're looking for budget cuts, either.

6. **Continuously Educate and Learn:** Make learning a core part of your organization's culture. Stay informed about emerging trends, new technologies, and shifts in consumer behavior. Encourage your team to pursue ongoing education and explore new ideas that could influence the future of the industry.

CHAPTER TEN

REPURPOSING OUR SUPERPOWER

"There's an answer / If you reach into your soul / And the sorrow that you know / Will melt away / And then a hero comes along / With the strength to carry on / And you cast your fears aside / And you know you can survive / So, when you feel like hope is gone / Look inside you and be strong / And you'll finally see the truth / That a hero lies in you."

–MARIAH CAREY,
"Hero," 1993

Mariah Carey is a fellow Long Islander, like me and also my best friend, Kristin, who was introduced in the dedication. Kristin had a beautiful and powerful singing voice, but she kept it under wraps. Until, one day, she decided to sing "Hero" on a recording meant for her father as inspiration during his battle with cancer in his fifties. It blew us all away, especially him. He's still alive as of the time of this writing and in his late-eighties, along with his wife, who is the same age.

Unfortunately, Kristin did not survive her battle with cancer, which is a tragic loss for all of us. Thankfully, her voice lives on in this recording to offer strength to others who believe in something but are struggling to achieve it. This industry has many heroes. The struggle is real, but it's worth it. I hope you'll feel inspired to carry on the mission, even when it's scary and hard, keeping in mind what that mission really is. **Life insurance rescues the lives that someone else leaves behind.** It does so in a unique way that is hard to compare to anything else.

As stated in Chapter One, the essence of the insurance industry is rooted in a superpower, which is a concept known as pooling. Pooling allows us to share risk among large groups of people, ensuring that when tragedy strikes, the burden doesn't fall on one person or one family alone. Traditionally, this superpower has been used to address financial risks, including the risk of dying too soon and even living too long. But what happens when we repurpose this superpower for a world facing new and evolving risks, taking other trends into consideration?

The landscape of risk itself is changing. Advances in medicine, shifting social norms, and the growing impact of climate change are creating new groups of people who need help managing their own individual risks. This chapter explores how the life insurance industry can repurpose its usage of pooling resources to address these emerging needs and remain relevant in a rapidly changing world.

NUANCE 20: Who Needs Our Help Now vs. Underwriting Them Out of the Pool

For decades, the life insurance industry has built its business model on identifying and underwriting risk. In simple terms, the goal has been to figure out who is most likely to die and either charge them more for coverage or exclude them from the pool altogether. However, as societal attitudes evolve and medical advancements change the nature of many once-deadly conditions, the industry must reconsider who it is excluding—and why.

WHAT'S HAPPENING WITH HIV, DIABETES, CANCERS, HEART DISEASE?

Take HIV, as an example. Not long ago, an HIV diagnosis was seen as a death sentence, and life insurers were quick to exclude individuals with HIV from coverage. Now, thanks to advances in antiretroviral therapies that have transformed HIV into a manageable chronic condition for many, that logic no longer applies. People with HIV are now living long, healthy lives, and the industry must reassess how it treats this group.

Similarly, diabetes, various forms of cancer, and heart disease are no longer automatic exclusions from life insurance. Medical advancements have improved survival rates and quality of life for individuals with these conditions. The industry must shift from viewing these individuals as uninsurable to finding ways to support them. The challenge is no longer about whether these people belong in the pool, but rather how we can pool resources to help them live longer and healthier lives.

WHAT RISKS MIGHT EMERGE WITH THE TRANSGENDER COMMUNITY?

Another emerging group that the life insurance industry must consider is the transgender community. Transgender individuals often face unique health challenges and disparities in healthcare access. Moreover, societal stigma and discrimination can exacerbate mental health issues and increase risks such as suicide.

The industry needs to approach this community with empathy and understanding. Instead of underwriting transgender individuals out of the pool due to perceived higher risks, insurers should focus on how they can provide meaningful protection and support for these individuals—and not just because it might be a law to do so.

Doing so includes addressing the specific needs of transgender people, from mental health care to gender-affirming medical procedures, and ensuring that life insurance products are inclusive and equitable.

WHAT ABOUT PEOPLE WHO LIVE IN CLIMATE CHANGE AFFECTED AREAS?

As I write this section, Florida has just been hit with two deadly and destructive hurricanes inside of two weeks (Helene and Milton). Climate change is rapidly altering the risk landscape of our industry, especially for those living in vulnerable areas. Whether it's an increased chance for flooding, wildfires, or hurricanes, people in these regions face heightened risks that traditional life insurance models may not adequately cover.

The industry needs to think beyond just geographic exclusions or higher premiums for those living in climate-prone areas. What if, instead, we pooled resources to help communities mitigate the risks of climate change or avoid loss? That could mean creating ideas that offer more than just financial protection for losses; it could also mean incentives for relocation and rebuilding. Regulators play a major role, and collaboration for solutions is intensely needed. This idea is not an attempt to solve the issue—because that would be a book in and of itself—but it is a plea to put the best minds on the task and work from a place of intent.

WHAT ABOUT RISING MENTAL ILLNESS?

Mental illness is becoming an increasingly significant issue worldwide, yet it remains one of the most stigmatized health challenges. The life insurance industry has historically been hesitant to cover individuals with severe mental health conditions, but as understanding and treatment of mental illness improves, so, too, must the industry's approach.

Insurers can pool resources together to support mental health initiatives, offering coverage that includes mental health treatment and providing resources for prevention and early intervention. By focusing on helping individuals manage and overcome their mental health challenges, the industry can play a vital role in reducing long-term risks instead of simply denying people coverage.

WHAT CAN WE PROVIDE IN ADDITION TO OR INSTEAD OF A LUMP SUM OF MONEY?

The traditional life insurance model revolves around providing a lump sum of money to beneficiaries after a policyholder's death. But as the nature of risk changes, so, too, should the solutions we offer. Instead of—or even in addition to—financial payouts, what if life insurance also provided access to health care, mental health services, or even relocation assistance for those affected by climate change?

Repurposing our superpower means thinking creatively about what people really need to feel secure. In some cases, money alone isn't enough. The industry needs to explore new ways of pooling together resources to create offerings that address the broader spectrum of risks people face today.

POOLING FOR LONGEVITY AND ACCESSING THE CURES FOR DREAD DISEASES

In an effort to promote repurposing the industry's superpower, I was inspired by what I learned from doing some deep innovation work for a pharmaceutical company that made devices. These are devices that put drugs into your body, not the drugs themselves.

However, at the time, more than 80% of their sales were for devices related to diabetes. What were they concerned about? They knew back in 2015 that the cure for diabetes would be less than ten years out, reducing the need for insulin and injectable drugs. *(We now know these as Mounjaro, Ozempic, Wegovy, etc.)* While we helped them to create strategies and frameworks for innovation within their company, I was stewing about something else.

I remember a story about the price of Epi-Pens, injection devices used to stop anaphylactic shock from allergies, such as peanuts, and prevent death. The manufacturers of the device justified a massive cost increase because the demand was high, and people need it. But that made it inaccessible to some and appalled many who felt that the manufacturer was being greedy at the expense of people's lives.

But, on the other hand, the price tag of inventing, testing, and approving a new drug is staggering, too. Doesn't the manufacturer deserve to get a return on investment? A dilemma, indeed.

Then, I thought about how society doesn't leave its weak behind and how the insurance industry was formed around passing the hat. In the case of drugs which are not covered by insurance–because it would drive rates too high–you might find people taking up collections for poor families in need of such drugs who can't afford them. Could the superpower of our industry be used in such a way?

Then, I thought of an idea. Perhaps one of the most innovative ways the industry can repurpose its superpower is by helping people access life-saving treatments. In a world where medical advancements are rapidly evolving, extending lives and curing diseases that were once fatal, life insurance could evolve from simply providing financial security to offering access to these breakthroughs.

I learned that not only was the cure for diabetes on the horizon *(now manifesting in many of the super expensive and hard to obtain weight loss and diabetes management drugs you see on the market today),* but so are cures for blindness, cancer, and other dreaded diseases.

NUANCE 21: Can Pooling Create a Different Financial Instrument in the Age of Advancing Tech?

How might we become the world's most sophisticated drug dealer? *(LOL!)*

Seriously, consider the concept of "Cure Futures." Instead of simply paying out a lump sum upon death, the life insurance industry could offer access to cutting-edge medical treatments that extend life and improve the quality of life for the consumers. Pooling resources for the purpose of living longer *and* healthier lives is a powerful way to repurpose life insurance's core function. It transforms the industry from one that reacts to death into one that proactively supports life.

New drugs have the potential to change the world for the better, but they often come with exorbitant price tags that limit the public's access to them. Pharmaceutical companies and their investors are entitled to earn a return on their investments, particularly when they're tackling diseases that were once considered incurable. However, when the cost of treatment reaches millions of dollars, it creates a significant barrier to accessibility, as seen with recent examples like a leukemia treatment costing nearly $1 million and gene therapies for vision loss and spinal muscular atrophy priced at hundreds of thousands to millions of dollars.

The challenge lies in balancing the cost of innovation with accessibility. Health insurers often hesitate to cover expensive new treatments, especially when these therapies don't fit neatly into existing pricing models. Additionally, a single claim for one of these high-cost drugs could drain much of an insurance pool, making them impractical to cover.

One potential solution is to introduce a financial model that resembles insurance but focuses on funding future cures. By allowing individuals to purchase contracts for access to treatments that are not yet available (i.e. "futures"), a large pool of people could contribute to funding the research needed to develop these cures. For example, if millions of people contributed $250 annually toward the development of a specific cure, it could generate billions of dollars to accelerate research while guaranteeing access to the treatment at a more set price once it's available. It doesn't have to be free, just affordable and reasonable.

This approach could supplement traditional health insurance, providing equal access to treatments regardless of a person's health status. Pharmaceutical companies would benefit from a steady flow of research funding, while consumers would have peace of mind knowing they have a pathway to potentially life-saving cures without facing financial ruin. Though it's a complex challenge, collaboration between drug companies, financial services, and healthcare providers could make these costly miracle cures more accessible to all.

It's a win for the pharma companies because they get money early, and it's a win for the consumer because they get to access live-saving medicines at a reasonable price—or they can transfer the privilege to someone else who needs it. Futures contracts can be created for just about anything if you can predict what the price will likely be in the future. When researchers are within spitting distance of a cure, these numbers should be attainable.

SCAN ME

Figure 25: This QR code will take you to the article in Stat Magazine describing Cure Futures

So, I wrote an article about it in 2018 and tested the idea. It wasn't picked up by any insurance industry magazines, but it was picked up by a pharma publication called *Stat*. This type of recognition made me proud, and I still think it's an idea worth pursuing.

However, to do so would require someone with a strong stomach to deal with all the red-tape, regulation, and so forth. But we cannot deny it any longer; Houston, we do have a problem. How will we use what we have to solve it?

MAKING IT CHEAP OR MAKING IT FAIR?

One of the challenges the industry faces when repurposing its superpower is the tension between making insurance affordable and making it fair. Traditionally, life insurance has focused on making coverage as accessible as possible by keeping premiums low. However, as we shift toward addressing more complex risks, fairness may need to take precedence over cost.

Fairness means pricing products based on the true level of risk, not just the ability of the policyholders to pay. For example, people living in climate-prone areas or those with chronic health conditions may need to pay higher premiums to reflect their higher risk. To offset those higher upfront costs, these premiums should come with additional benefits and protections that make the coverage worthwhile. It's about finding a balance between making insurance affordable and ensuring that everyone gets the coverage they need.

THE BIG TO-DO

Seek Emerging Problems and Determine If Pooling Is Helpful

Repurposing our superpower isn't just about reacting to changes in the risk landscape—it's about actively seeking out emerging problems and figuring out how pooling and sharing resources can help address them. The life insurance industry has a long history of solving problems that individuals can't handle on their own. Now, it's time to expand that mission to new areas and create new solutions.

Here are 5 big to-dos for the life insurance industry:

1. **Identify New Risk Groups:** Stay ahead of emerging trends by continuously identifying new groups of people who need protection. Whether it's individuals with chronic health conditions, vulnerable communities affected by climate change, or people facing rising mental health challenges, these groups represent opportunities for repurposing the industry's superpower of pooling together resources for the greater good.

2. **Think Beyond Money:** Consider what people really need to feel secure. In addition to financial payouts, think about how insurance can offer access to health care, relocation assistance, or other resources that help policyholders navigate life's challenges.

3. **Balance Affordability with Fairness:** Strive to make insurance both affordable and fair. That means pricing products based on the true level of risk while ensuring that everyone has access to the coverage and support they need.

4. **Proactively Solve Problems:** Don't wait for risks to become crises. Actively seek out emerging problems and explore how pooling resources can help address them. Whether it's finding new ways to cover mental health care or helping communities rebuild after natural disasters, the industry's superpower can be repurposed to tackle the challenges of tomorrow.

5. **Work with Influencers and Regulators:** If the problem is solvable but regulations are not aligned, use the tools of creative problem solving, empathy, listening, etc. to collaborate with constituents who have the power to make change. When enough people agree, miracles can happen.

All of these ideas are here to remind us that anything that's good for the world is possible if we want it badly enough *(or goodly enough).* My hope is that we do.

CONCLUSION

"The future never looked so near / As the ball drops, year after year."

–GARY SIRAK AND THE G. SIRAK BAND,

"All About the Snow," 2023

If you've gotten this far, I would like to thank you for reading the book and for your interest in this subject.

To conclude, this book contains a "cheat sheet" on the next page, which graphically summarizes all the nuances discussed, lays out the major imperatives, and supplies some helpful tools that were referenced. In addition, included is the grid that helps us do fairer comparisons to our category. Hopefully, it inspires you and your teams in new ways, helping everyone become more in tune with the subtleties that can potentially help us make more progress in the future than we have in the recent past.

If you are interested in exploring ideas or discussing any of these topics, I can be reached at maria@mariafs.com.

While I may not know you personally, I am sincerely hoping that whatever impact you are intending to make in this industry, that you feel strong and confident about achieving it. More power to you!

Let's make the future of the industry as vibrant and valuable as we can, while we still can!

UNFAIR COMPARISONS; NUANCING THE 'SOLD NOT BOUGHT' CATEGORY

Nuance Summary and Suggested Explorations

NUANCE #	SUGGESTED EXPLORATION
1. Product or Utility?	Who do you know that works for utility companies? Electricity, water, sanitation, tollways? Ask them how they deal with the issue of being taken for granted or under-appreciated. Listen for something new and useful!
2. Pennies from Heaven?	Talk to 25 people under the age of 30 and ask them how they think insurance "works." If they don't understand at all, explain the concept of pooling. Ask them to feed back to you what they learned. Note patterns.
3. What Problem Does It Solve? For Whom?	Convene a team to discuss and enumerate some of the biggest challenges today that can be solved through pooling and sharing but are not turned into insurance products? Consider what would happen if they were?
4. Profitable Enough?	Actuarial Experiment! (Internal). What would have to be true for your company to exit the life insurance business because of profit margin? How far are you from that line? If you're close, why is that so?
5. Need Does Not Equal Demand	Talk to the last 20-30 people who bought life insurance in your firm. Ask them what drove them to do it, not just to decide to do it, but to agree to go through the process. .Ask about those interactions with others that the agent wasn't involved in. Look for patterns.
6. Commissions as a % of What?	Explore 10 professions that get paid on commissions. Find out what's typical and how it's calculated. Find common ground for comparison purposes (such as % of dollars spent by the consumer over a period of time). Note if it changes attitudes about the amount agents get paid.
7. Physical and Emotional Threats Trigger The Same Behavior	Speak to 50 consumers and 50 agents. Ask the consumers what they are most concerned about when dealing with an insurance professional. Ask agents what makes them most apprehensive when approaching a new client. Dig deep. Show empathy. Listen.
8. Naysayers or Lack of Two-Way Exchange?	Speak to the last 25 people who said no because they didn't believe they need it or they don't believe in it. Be interested in them without an agenda for changing their mind. Probe in the areas that might suggest there is a need, but without judgement.
9. Non-Professionals' Opinions are Magical	Watch as many Tik Tok videos on the subject of life insurance that you can find. Look at the chat questions. Look for patterns and commonalities. Look for new dynamics that didn't exist before.
10. The Invisible Wall	Longitudinal Study: Track the Nos and Not Nows of 20 people. Agents may have to tell you who they are and allow you reach out about every 6 months or check data bases to see if they obtained life insurance. If they did, find out when, why, and how it happened. What happened in the moment they decided to act?

UNFAIR COMPARISONS; NUANCING THE 'SOLD NOT BOUGHT' CATEGORY

Nuance Summary and Suggested Explorations

11. It Takes a Village	Hire and observe a true Finder, Grinder, Binder and Minder team. Track 10 of their prospect's activities from every communication, appointment, sale, etc. Note patterns and be open to learning.
12. Shame, Judgment and Empathy	Leverage the Empathy Mad Lib. Gather a team of people to do the exercise together, see what stories people create. Engage with other empathy simulation tools such as personas, or storytelling methods.
13. Can't Automate Empathy	Check into 20 service scenarios where automation/AI prompted someone to use canned language or prompt to make someone feel good. Listen to recorded calls or read email responses that contain such language. Note how people respond.
14. Irrational vs. Rational	Map all the experiences of the client/customer (or for that matter, agents' experiences, too). Plot them on the spectrum of rational to irrational. Then note which ones are already automated or those that might be "over" automated.
15. Authenticity	Take every core communication piece and ask someone outside your organization to objectively benchmark it using the Authenticity Scoring Tool. Note which ones score the lowest. Make improvements.
16. Where is Tech Messing it Up?	Look at every part of the application, underwriting, service, and claims experience. Look for the places where automation breaks the promises or messes up the work of the human.
17. A Recipe for Fairness	Look at the attribute list on page 158. Convene a team of thinkers to determine 3 industries that provide a fairer comparison. Invite professionals from these industries to visit with your team. Ask them to weigh in on your biggest challenges.
18. Not All Innovation is Equal	Use the innovation portfolio tool as a n exercise for your team. Plot every initiative you have in flight and see how the balance is. If it's off balance, look for new ways to bring it in balance.
19. What Do We Take for Granted?	Rally your craziest, most creative thinkers. The ones that make some people's eyes roll. The ones that others may label a dreamer. Hold a session where you list all of the assets/attributes of your model that you believe will always be true. Invent scenarios under which they are no longer true.
20. Who Needs Our Help?	Rally a team of thinkers. Come up with groups of people with certain needs, characteristics, or problems that pooling or probabilistic thinking could potentially help.
21. Can Pooling Create Different Financial Instruments?	Ideate on other ways in which pooling resources can create better outcomes. Consider the advances in technology that make things that were not knowable before, knowable.

UNFAIR COMPARISONS; NUANCING THE "SOLD, NOT BOUGHT" CATEGORY

Imperatives, Tools, and a Guide to Fairer Comparisons

THE 5 BIGGEST TO DO'S
(Imperatives)

1. Engage Teams with the "Why" and the Superpower of the industry
2. Empathy Training
3. Shifting from Sales Tactics to Fear Management
4. Creative Problems Solving/ Problem Reframing Training (Design Thinking)
5. Get Inspired By Fairer Comparisons

TOOL-BOX
(Use QR Code for Downloadable PDFs)

1. 5 Whys
2. The Innovation Portfolio
3. The Empathy Mad Lib
4. The Authenticity Scoring Tool
5. The Guide to Fairer Comparisons

SCAN ME

www.ingramcontent.com/pod-product-compliance
Ingram Content Group UK Ltd.
Pitfield, Milton Keynes, MK11 3LW, UK
UKHW020511061026
15625UKWH00039B/801/J

9 798992 334807